W

THE GODS
AND SYMBOLS
OF ANCIENT
EGYPT

D0089267

MANFRED LURKER

THE GODS AND SYMBOLS OF ANCIENT EGYPT

AN ILLUSTRATED DICTIONARY

with 114 illustrations

THAMES AND HUDSON

Contents

'Egypt, though it borders upon Libya, is not a region abounding in wild animals. The animals that do exist in the country, whether domesticated or otherwise, are all regarded as sacred. If I were to explain why they are consecrated to the several gods, I should be led to speak of religious matters, which I particularly shrink from mentioning.'

Herodotus, History, Book 2, 65.

Introduction to the World of Egyptian Symbolism

The spiritual world of the ancient Egyptians is not immediately understandable by the western civilizations of the twentieth century. Magical and symbolic images exist side by side and are often inextricably interwoven one with the other. Siegfried Schott speaks plainly of 'symbol and magic as the primary forms of ancient Egyptian thought'. Even affairs of state were determined by symbolic magic and pronouncements of a mythical nature. In all our considerations we must not forget that our reasoned logic would be alien to the inhabitant of the Nile valley. He did not live in a world of concepts but in a world of images. This world of the Egyptians appears to us to contradict itself, but this is only because we cannot apply the standards of that age to ourselves.

We may find it ridiculous for artists to represent the sky as a cow, or for a beetle to be venerated as a symbol of the sun god, but in past ages, among peoples having a mythical view of the world, the formative principle was not of logic but of an outlook governed by images. Like the sun that sets in the west, to begin its renewed journey in the morning, the dead are buried in the western part of the country so that they may also gain new life. The whole symbolic evocation rests upon the supposed, and in the end actual, correspondence of things, on the relationship between microcosm and macrocosm as intuitively understood by the mind and visually by the eye. For the men of ancient times the world was no less a totality than it is for us; more precisely speaking, the universe presents us with no fewer enigmas than it did men in ancient and classical times. Furthermore, the 'coming of age of the world' – the expansion of our intellectual horizons – is only relative. Modern man tries to comprehend the world by measurement and calculation; he dissects, he analyses. The ancient Egyptians, the Babylonians, and to some extent the Greeks, used images; their view of the world was a comprehensive one. Before man tried to count the stars he grouped them into images. Thus the star-studded firmament became one of the most compelling picture-books of mankind. This imaginative world led man towards the divine, to the meaning of existence, and he tried to portray this meaning by the use of images.

In the last analysis symbols are unreal and abstract for they go beyond the bounds of concrete form. It would be wrong to suppose that the man who reasons in symbols necessarily takes his symbols for reality. It is likely, however, that he sees an image in everything which he can immediately observe. The man with a magical view of the world has a different standpoint; he sees the image and its original as one, therefore the symbol is reality. To him the colour red not only symbolizes life but it is imbued with life and may make possible resurrection after death. A man's name does not only serve to identify him but is a component part of his very being; to deface the name is to bring harm to the man who bears it. In the Pyramid Texts the hieroglyph for 'snake' was pierced with several knives and many animals shown without their legs, all of which were meant to render a dangerous animal harmless. All Egyptian magic was rooted in the belief in a secret force which produced a supernatural effect; the Egyptians called this *Hekau*. This power was part of the nature of the gods but could also be employed by experts such as the mortuary priest whose task it was to exorcise the powers of death and secure a continued existence thereafter for the deceased.

Magic and Religion need not be mutually exclusive just because the concepts of the former belong more to a determined view of the world, while religion concerns the relationship of man to god, for as conceptions of the divine nature differ so world views also differ. It is possible to make fundamental distinctions between the magical, mythical and rational outlooks, which have been compared to sleeping, dreaming and the waking state. Magical reasoning is found especially among people who have no written language, who know that all phenomena are linked by a 'participation mystique'. With the advent of writing, and written culture, a transition to mythical reasoning usually occurs. Man ceases to see the world as a synthesis and regards himself as involved in cosmic polarity. Myth displays the liberation of the self from the environment; for the first time man experiences space and time. For the ancient Egyptians myths were the 'doings of the gods at the beginning of the world but these events were symbols expressing the present organization of things' (Clark 1959, 261). The god of the air, Shu, separates heaven (Nut) and earth (Geb), a symbolic act denoting a consciousness of up and down, light and darkness, good and evil. Even when magical reasoning is suppressed in the mythical world view, it is nevertheless still an effective force that finds expression even in our rationalistic world.

The first expression of this magical world view in the land of the Nile occurred in art in the geometric ornamentation of the Neolithic Period. The herringbone pattern from the Lower Egyptian site of Merimde and the black pots of the Upper Egyptian Tasian culture, the latter scored with lines filled with white paste, did not only 'originate from the limitations of the material and technology by virtue of man's innate urge towards artistic style and imitation'. This ornamentation is better understood as symbolic.

All Egyptian culture was of religious origin. Astronomy arose from the need to maintain the timing necessary for ritual, i.e. the rising of Sothis, the phases of the moon. The oldest maps concerned the 'geography of the beyond'; they were painted on the bottom of coffins as signposts to the next world. Doctors mostly belonged to the priestly class. There were laws in the form of religious commandments for hygiene and prevention of disease. State administration was determined by the concept of divine kingship – to serve Pharaoh was to serve God. Judicial officials bore the title 'priest of Maat'. Laws were given by the creator god himself and secured by the king. To understand the fine arts one must begin from their religious origin. The purpose of Egyptian art was not so much to satisfy one's aesthetic sense but to fulfil the objectives of cult and magic. To be precise, one cannot speak of art in the western sense. The statues of the Pyramid Age and the painting in Theban tombs must not be regarded totally as reproductions of visible reality for they were not meant to be copies but symbols.

The well known fact that Egyptian art is faithful to tradition is also of significance for the understanding of symbolic motifs. Even the art of the Amarna Age with its specific motifs was not so innovative as one might think. Eric Hornung has shown that even the typical motifs of that period, e.g. the extended arms of the sun, are already present in the Middle Kingdom, not in iconography but as an image in literature. In general, the content and form of Egyptian art were at no time totally fixed but were capable of modification despite rigidity. The image of the 'winged panther' was both a symbol of heaven and of the sun. The morning sun was regarded as a falcon in its aspect of son and the evening sun was seen as a man in its aspect of father. According to Wolfgang Westendorf, the original image of the 'flying panther' developed into the 'flying sun' (winged disc). Precious stones, the lotus flower, the frog, the heron, the boat and the pyramid moved the soul of the Egyptian who saw below the surface of things, thereby encountering the eternal. Therefore a wealth of symbolic motifs confront anyone who studies Egyptian religion and art. Since the purpose of all true symbols is to direct the individual away from the superficial concerns of life towards the centre of existence, all symbolic phenomena fall into a few typical categories. All symbolism crystallizes around the poles of existence, around coming into being and passing away, light and darkness, good and evil. The true symbol always points beyond the here and now for it is a signpost to another world. All lower things direct the mind symbolically to something higher, each fragment points to the whole and everything ephemeral is an image of the eternal.

Although a part can indicate the whole (*pars pro toto*), it can never replace it, for a symbol is always subsidiary to that to which it refers. The purpose of symbols is not to reveal the hidden relationships between earthly phenomena in a rationalistic way but rather to point to the irrational. Knowledge of cosmic order was one of the secrets which were withheld from the profane. The title 'Master of Secrets', common in the Old Kingdom, is to be understood in this way. A symbol is meant to direct the initiate to something higher and to reveal it to him at the same time, but it must also conceal this from the ignorant. Knowledge of the meaning of images was not accessible to everyone. Let us take as an example the title 'Master of the secrets of the royal robing room'. He was not only one of the few who knew how and on what occasion the various items of the royal vestments were to be donned, he also knew where each individual garment or piece of jewellery was placed according to myth: the act of dressing was in itself a symbolic act.

A symbol has manifold significance and therefore its origin and purpose cannot often be explained satisfactorily. Sometimes the symbol seems to contradict itself. There are, in fact, symbols which refer to both poles of existence: life and death, good and evil. We often encounter this ambivalence in the land of the Nile. Osiris, for example, was regarded as a god of the netherworld and also simultaneously as Lord of Heaven; he was the setting and the rising sun; he could be killed by his brother Seth, and yet be immortal.

This ambivalent nature is especially apparent with some female deities. The goddess Bastet could appear as a friendly cat who was fêted by women with music and dance. The same goddess, however, under the name of

Sekhmet, appeared as a gruesome devourer, a bloodthirsty lady of slaughter with the head of a lioness.

On first acquaintance with the barely intelligible mass of symbolic phenomena one may well imagine that symbols are created involuntarily and according to individual differences. Contradicting this is the fact that symbols are not confined to time and place, but to a large extent follow certain rules independent of ethnic tradition and religion. Psychologists have established that images do not only approach man from the visible world but also exist in the depths of his own soul, the unconscious. The Swiss psychologist Carl Gustav Jung has called these images archetypes. These may still appear to the individual today in dreams or in semi-consciousness. Archetypes enter the conscious mind in the form of symbols and myths. Thus the symbols of the cat and the lion belong to the 'great mother' archetype, she who gives birth and who devours, the earth goddess from whom all life comes and to whom all life returns. Since archetypes exist in the souls of all men, they can enter surface consciousness in all nations at all times. Well known archetypes from other religions, those of the magna mater, the god on earth, the water of life, the sacred chest and the road to the other world, are also found in the realm of ancient Egyptian ideas and imagery.

The archetype of the god on earth was clearly expressed in royal symbolism. According to mythical tradition individual gods had ruled over the land of the Nile in primeval times. Special significance was attributed to Osiris, son of the earth god, Geb, and the sky goddess, Nut. 'Scarcely had he become king when he raised the Egyptian people from their miserable and barbarous existence, caused them to learn about the fruits of the earth, gave them laws and taught them to respect the gods' (Posener 1962, 203). After the death of Osiris his son Horus succeeded him as king of Egypt. All Egyptian royal symbolism was founded on the complementary ideas that Osiris was the last dead king and Horus the king 'on the throne of the living'. Thus each royal rule must have appeared to the simple believer as the rule of a god king. To his subjects the king was the visible incarnation of the god Horus.

As the successor of Osiris, who once ruled over mortal men, the king became Osiris at his life's end. After the Fourth Dynasty the king additionally became designated as the son of the sun-god Re or simply as his father's 'living image on earth'. The temple of Amenhetep III at Luxor shows how the sun-god, this time Amun, assumed the form of the reigning king and consorted with the queen. In this way the divine succession of the next ruler was assured. A last, albeit very weak, echo of this archetype is found in the theory of the divine right of kings in western monarchies.

Since the Egyptian king was not only a central figure in political history but also in religious life, we should consider him and his attendant symbolism closely. A new era began with each new king, each accession was the repetition of three mythical and historical events: the introduction of prosperity and order by Osiris, the triumph of Horus over his enemy who wanted to take the government of Egypt from him, and lastly, the unification of Upper and Lower Egypt. The vulture of the Upper Egyptian town of El Kab and the uraeus (snake) of Buto in the Delta were regarded as the heraldic animals of the Two Lands. On the three coffins and the gold face mask of the young pharaoh Tutankhamun we see the vulture and uraeus on the brow

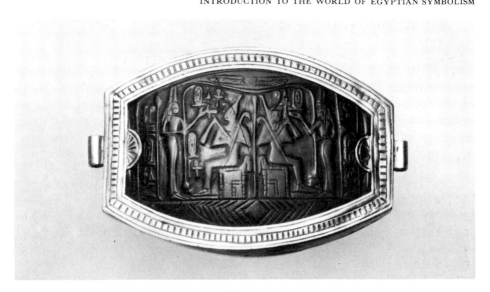

A carnelian bracelet plaque of Amenhetep III (1417–1379 BC). It is one of five known made to celebrate the pharaoh's jubilee, probably his first in his thirtieth regnal year. The scene shows part of the *heb-sed* ceremonies with Amenhetep seated within the twin Pavilions of Festival. On the left he wears the White Crown of Upper Egypt, and on the right, the Red Crown of Lower Egypt. Queen Tiy stands before him offering an ankh (life) and the symbol for 'hundreds of thousands of years'. On either side of the scene his titles are given in full, hailing him as 'The beneficient god, Lord of the Two Lands' who is given life for eternity. The gold mounts are modern settings copying the style of ancient examples. Metropolitan Museum of Art, New York, Carnarvon Collection, 1926.

symbolizing the Two Lands. As a sacred animal the vulture was identified with the goddess Nekhbet who symbolized the White Crown of Upper Egypt, while the uraeus referred to Wadjet who was identified with the Red Crown of Lower Egypt. Thus in the two heraldic animals, in the crowns and in the two goddesses, was expressed the dualistic conception of the ancient Egyptians, namely, that the world perceived through the senses had arisen from the division of an original unity.

Whereas in Greek mythology there was much traffic from the regions of the gods to that of mortals, in Egyptian religion these realms were sharply divided. There was only one major link, and that was through the king. Hitherto we have purposely avoided the term 'Pharaoh'. In the Old and Middle Kingdoms *pr-'з* meant the royal palace (literally 'the great house'). From the Eighteenth Dynasty onwards the king himself was also designated in this way, and from the Twenty-second Dynasty the word was employed as a title in front of the royal name. The rites performed at the king's accession were full of symbolism. First, the candidate for the throne was purified with the water of life, 'that he might become young like Re', who also cleansed himself before he embarked on his journey across the heavens. On the evening before the day of the coronation the so-called djed-pillar was erected. This was probably a fertility rite. The coronation itself, according to extant reliefs, was performed by the gods. After the coronation the king shot an arrow towards the cardinal points of the compass, with which he symbolically assumed rulership of the world.

The king secured earthly and cosmic order. Like the gods he was the bearer of life, the symbol of which, the ankh (*crux ansata*), he held in his hands. On his diadem or crown he wore the golden snake (uraeus), symbol of the fiery eye of the sun which destroyed all the enemies of the light. Usually at the end of the pharaoh's first thirty years of reign, and at shorter intervals thereafter, he needed a renewed supply of divine power. To achieve this the *heb-sed* festival was celebrated. 'It seems that a statue of the king was buried on the evening before, but this rite was given a new interpretation. It could well be that we have the remains of ritual regicide in these the most ancient scenes of the jubilee festival' (Helck 1956, 164). The ritual murder of the king was also performed among other Nilotic peoples, as in the kingdom of Meroe, where the priests determined the time of the sacrifice into Ptolemaic times (Wainwright 1937). If one regards ritual regicide as a sacrificial death, then there is a full awareness of the significance of the word. A people offered its most precious possession, hoping thereby to gain a new vital force. Since new life had issued from the murdered god Osiris, the king also, through his death, was to secure the continued stability of his people. At the jubilee the prehistoric custom of killing the king was transformed into a rite for prolonging his life. The fact that the festival took place thirty years after the accession could be based on the thirty-year revolution of Saturn which was the outermost known planet orbiting the sun. In ancient southern India ritual regicide took place after twelve years' reign, in this case the revolution of the planet Jupiter was the deciding factor. Frobenius himself has proved in the case of culturally less advanced peoples that the position of the constellations was decisive in determining the time for the ritual death. In Kordofan in the Sudan all fires were extinguished until the new king was installed on the throne. With the death of the ruler law and order (symbolized by the flame) perished. Seen in this way the ceremony of 'lighting the fire' received its special significance at the Egyptian *heb-sed*; the king himself kindled a new fire and so ensured light and life.

To conclude this introduction to the world of ancient Egyptian symbols there must be a direct warning against wanting to read a subconscious meaning into every text. Considerations of Egyptian art and religion show numerous hoaxes and false evaluations. Men of classical times had already applied their own standards to the material found in the land of the Nile; aware of its antiquity they were unable to understand or accept its symbolic concepts and imagery. Horapollo's conception of hieroglyphs in the fourth century AD as purely symbolic characters, and at the same time the expression of profound thoughts, gave impetus to the hieroglyphic studies of the Renaissance. Under the cloak of learned authority these notions infiltrated into Europe from Egypt mostly in the form of fanciful conceptions. As Hermes Trimegistos, Thoth entered into the intellectual and spiritual life of the West: hermetic doctrines fertilized alchemy, Rosicrucianism, Freemasonry and Theosophy. With awakened interest in archaeological research among wider circles, new fantasies appeared, for example, the legend of Pharaoh's curse, and the mystical theory of numbers attributed to the pyramid of Khufu, although numerous scientific publications have produced counter-arguments and refuted these 'theories' time and time again.

The Cultural and Religious History of Egypt

During the European Ice Age the Nile valley was probably a sparsely inhabited swamp area. With the gradual expansion of the deserts of North Africa the nomadic tribes, following the water sources, reached the fertile strip of the Nile, where they came into contact with Neolithic farming cultures. One of the most ancient peasant Neolithic cultures which has been studied is named after the site of Merimde on the western Delta edge. The people lived in oval huts of reeds and clay. The material culture consisted of stone tools, jewellery of stone beads, bone and ivory, and hand-made pottery (without the use of the wheel) which was occasionally decorated with a pattern resembling herringbone. The dead were buried within the settlement, sometimes under the floors of the dwellings, in the crouched, foetal position. This mode of burial, in which the dead remained with the living, was probably one origin of the characteristically Egyptian concept of the tomb as the home. The discoveries of a human figure of baked clay and a bull's head are of special interest and can be connected with Predynastic and Early Dynastic small amuletic bulls' heads, and with the later historical bull cults. The female statuettes which occur in the rather later Badarian culture of Upper Egypt tell much about the history of religion. These were naked and invariably the genitalia were especially emphasized. Here we have prehistoric evidence for the concept of the great mother goddess whose cult and iconography were distributed throughout the ancient Near East, and who later combined with the divine figures of Hathor and Isis, living on in them.

In their imagistic language the Egyptians called their land 'the Black Land and the Red Land'. The Black Land (*Kmt*) was the fertile area inundated annually by the Nile, depositing the fertile silt. In ancient times rainfall was already poor, therefore Egypt was not unjustly called 'the gift of the Nile'. The Delta, covered with picturesque swamp thickets, was the home of the papyrus plant and lotus flower, both of which influenced the shape of columns in Egyptian architecture. The Red Land (*Dšrt*) was a metaphorical name for the infertile sun-baked desert, the mountains of which can be seen beyond and above the fertile land as a pale strip to the east and west. The Egyptians denoted everything which was not part of the Valley with the same word and wrote it with the hieroglyphic determinative for 'hill country', whether referring to foreign lands or to the desert. This contrast in the nature of the country is reflected in mythological duality. Osiris, the god of fertility, contrasted with Seth, the god of the desert. Osiris, who gave mankind the fruits of the earth and the laws of heaven, was murdered by his brother, the sinister Seth. Yet new seed sprouted from the corpse of Osiris, as many scenes from pharaonic times show. The people traditionally made little figures of Osiris from Nile mud and sowed seeds of grain in them. The sprouting of the seeds was a symbol of reawakening after death. Like the god, the Egyptian soil died each year under the searing summer sun to produce renewed and luxuriant vegetation after the dry season and the ensuing inundation of the Nile, which was the water of life. One must be extremely careful when making mythological comparisons, but the ill-matched brothers Seth and Osiris bear many similarities to Cain and Abel. It is perhaps possible that symbolic motifs were formed, whether consciously or unconsciously, from the antagonism between the nomadic herding population and the settled agriculturalists in the land of the Nile. It could be that other mutually contradictory funerary beliefs began with this contrast; the tumulus surmounted by a stele, characteristic of nomadic peoples, is just as much a prototype for Egyptian tombs as is the house-shaped tombs of the settlers.

The regular cycle of the seasons, in which seedtime and harvest alternated in endless succession, coupled with the continual battle between the Nile floods and the desert sand, all contributed towards giving the spiritual life of the ancient Egyptian its characteristic form. He venerated the divine powers which made the fruits of the earth flourish and caused his cattle to increase, and he feared the uncanny forces which destroyed his seed, killed his herds and threatened his own life. Soon he grew from wondering at the existence and behaviour of things towards inquiring into their growth and decay. Above the black and the red land was the vault of the sky in which the sun was visible by day and the moon and stars by night. Did they not make manifest the bright and dark sides of life?

The belief in the kingdom of the dead lying in the west had two foundations. The first was the sunset, symbol of death, and the second was the desert to the west of the Nile valley in which all life perishes. The most important areas for burial were, therefore, situated on the west bank of the Nile, the pyramids at Giza, Abusir, Dahshur, etc., and the tombs of the nobles in the Theban necropolis and the Valley of the Kings a thousand years later. The earliest Neolithic burials, discovered at the Upper Egyptian site of Deir el Tasa, have the body laid on a north–south axis and on its left side so that the head faced west, towards the land of the dead. After the start of the Old Kingdom the dead faced east where the unconquerable light of the sun showed itself at the end of every night. At the beginning of the Eighteenth Dynasty the body was laid along an east–west axis with the eyes facing the rising sun and the head to the west, a symbolic reference to the entry of the deceased into the realm of the dead (Bonnet 1952, 564).

Concepts of death and the world beyond may easily be followed in the texts. In the Old Kingdom there were the Pyramid Texts, the main theme of which, with individual variations, was the existence of the king in the Beyond. Many spells from the Pyramid Texts were assimilated into the Coffin Texts which were painted onto the wooden sarcophagi of the Middle Kingdom. After the New Kingdom a papyrus with selected chapters from the so-called Book of the Dead was placed in the tomb with the deceased. Some of these chapters were derived from the corpus of spells in the Coffin Texts. In the Pyramid Texts the goal was the journey to heaven but in the New Kingdom the idea of the netherworld as the land of the dead had asserted itself.

The burial hall in the tomb of Ramesses VI (1156–1148 BC), no. 9 in the Valley of the Kings at Thebes. In the centre are the remains of the shattered granite sarcophagus (the pharaoh's mummy was found in 1898 in the cache hidden in the tomb of Amenhetep II, no. 35). The walls of the burial hall, and of the corridors leading to it, are covered with texts relating to the netherworld. On the astronomical ceiling the goddess Nut is represented twice (for day and night), her elongated body running down the centre with the sun disc shown travelling through her stomach in one representation and stars through the other.

Along with collections of spells which are independent in themselves (i.e., Pyramid Texts, Coffin Texts, Book of the Dead), the books of the netherworld (also called 'guides to the beyond') are of significance. These were painted on the walls of the royal tombs. Word and picture have coalesced in them to become as one. The central theme is the sun god's nightly journey through the netherworld and his rejuvenation, in which the dead king participated when he travelled through the Beyond. The earliest book concerning the netherworld, the sole one of its kind until the time of Akhenaten, was the 'Amduat' ('that which is in the duat', i.e., the netherworld). Until about the close of the New Kingdom these books of the netherworld were used as royal funerary texts, but as a result of democratizing tendencies they found their way onto the coffins and into the papyri of private individuals. It is significant that the iconography of Amduat and the 'Book of the Gates' depicts the sun as part of a picture containing the divine barque, whereas in the 'Book of Caverns' and the 'Book of the Earth' it is represented by a disc.

The three most important 'celestial images' can probably be traced back to the environment of the various nomes (administrative districts). On the coast the sky was perhaps regarded as a sea on which the sun god travelled in a boat. To others, dwelling perhaps in the inner Delta, the sky goddess was an enormous cow (Hathor) who planted her four legs as pillars on the corners of the earth and whose belly was the only part visible to diminutive man. To the third group, the desert dwellers, it was a woman (Nut) who stood arched on her hands and feet in order to give birth to the young sun in the east each morning.

The earliest form in which the State consolidated itself was through the unification of neighbouring tribes into nomes. Each nome had religious autonomy, worshipping a divine being who was symbolically represented on a 'standard' consisting of a pole and crossbeam. The hieroglyph for nome $(sp(3)t)$ represents a tract of land crossed by straight canals. The earliest title for the nome administrator literally meant 'he who excavates canals', an indication of the fact that irrigation was an important factor in the formation of the State in an almost rainless land. The thirty-eight original nomes were later increased to forty-two in order that they might correspond to the forty-two judges of the dead who assisted Osiris. All Egyptian nomes lay on the Nile which runs on a north–south axis. Egyptian farmers conceived of the river as a divine benefactor. The Nile and its personification were called Hapi. The inundation, so important for a good harvest, was celebrated with song and offerings as the 'coming of Hapi'. Since the interplay of male and female forces was necessary for all fertility, the Nile was repeatedly represented as a hermaphrodite, a man with female breasts.

Egypt only had two neighbours, the desert and the sea, thus an oasis culture in the truest sense of the word was able to form because of her seclusion from the rest of the world. Nevertheless, the land of the Nile did not lead the life of a recluse; at all times in her history she had contact with other peoples. In the Archaic Period the Egyptian nation already displayed the character of a land which lay on an intersection, on an isthmus between two continents. In the fourth millennium BC three races can be identified: the small, gracile Mediterranean race; a somewhat taller and more robust Cro-Magnon race, traces of which are found in the rest of North Africa; and a negroid race, which is not to be confused with true negroes. At the start of historic times in the Thinite Period the members of a brachycephalic race entered the scene. They were numerous and, although insignificant, are perhaps a tangible indication of the contact with Mesopotamia which can be authenticated at this time and also be observed in artistic influences.

We often come across dualism between Upper and Lower Egypt in Egyptian history. According to tradition king Menes united the hitherto rival lands. He is the first ruler who steps out of the obscurity of the Archaic Period into the light of history. As 'Lord of the Two Lands' he wore his own White Crown of Upper Egypt, together with the Red Crown of Lower Egypt. Wherever the hieroglyph for 'land' appeared in duplicate it meant 'Egypt' (the Two Lands).

The papyrus was used as the heraldic plant of the north, while a kind of flowering reed, also called the lily, stood for the south. The dualism of Upper and Lower Egypt was also apparent in social structure; the sparse grasslands

The slate palette of Narmer. At the top, flanked by two Hathor heads, the king's name appears in a serekh. The king himself is shown below wearing the Red Crown of Lower Egypt and with his name incorporating the scorpion hieroglyph before his face. Behind him, at much smaller size as convention demanded, walks his sandal bearer. In front of him four nome standards are carried, signifying his victory over his enemies who are shown decapitated with their heads between their feet. Dominating the centre of the palette are two entwined serpo-pards held on leashes. Their necks form a hollow between them, the area in which cosmetics such as green kohl paint would have been crushed, indicating the original use of the palettes before they became highly decorated ritual objects. Animals such as these serpo-pards show the early influence of Mesopotamian art in the Nile valley. At the bottom of the palette the king is represented as a mighty bull, battering down the walls of enemy cities. Amongst the royal titles of the pharaoh was 'The Horus, the Strong Bull, appearing in Right, Lord of the North and the South'. From Hierakonpolis, *c.* 3100 BC. Egyptian Museum, Cairo.

The slate palette of Narmer. Hathor heads flank the king's name in a serekh at the top. The figure of the king, wearing the tall White Crown of Upper Egypt, dominates this side of the palette. He holds a mace aloft in his right hand, about to smite a captive held in his left. This is a symbolic stance that appeared continually in Egyptian art right down to Roman times when even the Roman emperors in the guise of pharaohs are shown similarly smiting their enemies. At the back of the king's kilt is clearly shown the symbolic bull's tail; it is part of a *besau* or protective bead apron worn only by the pharaoh in the earliest times, although it was appropriated by commoners of high rank in the Middle Kingdom and up until the end of the Second Intermediate Period.

The king's diminutive sandal bearer is in attendance behind him and before him Horus, as a falcon above a stylized representation of papyrus, holds another victim ready for the king by a rope passed through the captive's nostrils. At the bottom of the palette two of the king's enemies are either fleeing, or possibly shown drowning. Their city is represented to the left, small, and surrounded by the so-called 'palace façade'. From Hierakonpolis, *c.* 3100 BC. Egyptian Museum, Cairo.

of the south mainly supported nomadic cattle herders who played the more active part in the formation of the Egyptian State, having subjugated the arable farmers of the north. Various items of royal dress, such as the crook, the so-called flail, the bull's tail and also the king's head-cloth (*nemes*) are all perhaps relics of a nomadic culture.

We must now return to the briefly mentioned Asiatic influence. Emigrants from Western Asia had already given the Egyptian language its Semitic elements long before historic times. The language which we know lies midway between Semitic and Hamitic. At the end of the fourth millennium in the Naqada II culture, named after the site near Thebes, there are some remarkable parallels with the Sumerian culture in Mesopotamia. Among these are representations of a certain type of ship (the *belem*, the prow and stern of which rise up almost vertically), and groups of heraldic animals, for example, the big 'cats' with snake-like necks of the Narmer palette which vanished from Egyptian iconography as quickly as they had appeared. Whether the cylinder seals which were discovered with some bodies are of Mesopotamian origin is as yet unresolved. Some Egyptologists, for example, Alexander Scharff, think it possible that hieroglyphic writing was influenced by Sumerian picture writing which had been invented shortly before. Fundamental connections between the Nile valley and the area of Western Asia and their obvious expression in art have moved into great prominence in the field of research since the Second World War, especially with the work of William Stevenson Smith in his *Interconnections in the Ancient Near East* (London, 1965).

The Hyksos invasion in the seventeenth century constituted a late surge of Asiatic influence. Their racial origin has not yet been identified; one can only be sure that they were an offshoot of the great migration of Western Asiatic peoples into whose sphere of influence the Hittites came and also the Kassites who occur in Babylonia. Through Hyksos influence new weapons, the horse, the chariot, and certain ornamental forms reached Egypt. The chief god of the Hyksos, called Baal, also of Syrian origin, was equated by the Egyptians with Seth. Syria was conquered in the Eighteenth Dynasty, which paved the way for the introduction of Syrian material culture, such as musical instruments, and divine images of Syrian type, Astarte the goddess of love, and Qadesh, who was mostly represented naked.

Let us consider some of the especially prominent deities in Egypt. Right back into the Archaic Period two groups of gods may be identified. First, there are the gods who were linked to a particular place, the old nome gods who were symbolized as an animal or an animal head. At Dendera for example, Hathor was venerated as a cow, Thoth as an ibis at Hermopolis and the ram-headed Khnum was regarded as 'Lord of Elephantine'. Gods which were not bound to a particular locality represented the various cosmic elements and phenomena and were usually shown in human form. Among these are the sky-goddess, Nut, the earth god, Geb, the god of vegetation, Osiris, and the creator god, Ptah. The theriomorphic (animal-shaped) gods belonged to North African Hamitic culture, while the anthropomorphic ones were connected with the concepts of the Western Semites.

At the beginning of the Old Kingdom the king was already regarded as the incarnation of the falcon-god Horus. He was seen as one upon whom the gods had bestowed the crown – in fact, he *was* a god. The name of the deity Horus had first place in the royal titular in order to proclaim this fact. After the Fifth Dynasty Horus was overtaken by Re, the sun-god. The new State god's supremacy in the Egyptian pantheon was due to the priests of On, the Heliopolis of the Greeks. At once the king was regarded as the bodily son of Re and Re's cult symbol, the obelisk, spread throughout the land.

Amenemhet I of the Twelfth Dynasty advanced the Theban god Amun to the position of new State god. He was also accessible to the simple classes of society in his animal manifestations as a ram and a Nile goose. In the theological system of his priesthood, however, he was the 'invisible one', the soul (*ba*) of all things. The names of Egyptian gods could be described as words with symbolism. It is very probable that the divine names originated for fear of pronouncing the real name, a name taboo as with the Hebrews. On the other hand, Egyptian names aptly described their owners. Amun was the 'hidden one', originally a god of the wind, Khons was the 'traveller', who crossed heaven as the moon-god, whilst the name of Isis may be derived from the 'throne' which she originally embodied and which is part of her name in hieroglyphs. Under the pharaohs Tuthmosis III and Amenhetep II a rationalistic spiritual outlook became apparent which contrasted on the other hand with a rigid dogma. Both perhaps sparked off Akhenaten's serious attempt at reform, in which only one god survived, Aten, whose symbol was the sun-disc. This monotheism, however, carried little weight with the Egyptian nation with its multifarious religious sensibilities, and it ran into bitter opposition from the Amun priesthood. After the death of the 'heretic king' the restoration caused spiritual life to be once again beset by torpor.

Osiris, who had been ruler of the dead since the end of the Old Kingdom, stepped more strongly into the foreground under the Ramessides. His myth made him more human and more tangible than either Re or Amun. With this dying and resurrected god was linked the hope for individual survival after death. When Egypt's position as a great power declined magic took over. What could not be effected by human effort or prayers and offerings to the gods would, one hoped, be achieved through sorcery.

In the Late Period animal cults became increasingly popular. Up to then sacred animals had only been viewed as manifestations of gods, or simply as their symbols, but in the first millennium BC the animals themselves became objects of veneration. This was the age, as the Greek historian Herodotus reports, when an Egyptian would let the flames consume his property but would stake his own life to save a sacred cat from the conflagration. At that time the cult of the Apis bull gained special significance. He had been a fertility symbol in the Thinite Period and his circle of worshippers, which spread out from his original cult centre in Memphis, soon embraced all Egypt. Persian, Ptolemaic and Roman times saw the growth of the prestige of Isis who was rich in magic arts and who once succeeded by cunning, in discovering the name of the highest god, thereby gaining power over all the world. As the faithful wife and exemplary mother, Isis became the most popular goddess. Her mysteries spread throughout the whole Mediterranean area in classical times, and even as far as Roman Britain where there was a temple dedicated to her in London.

It is not possible to expand here on the history of how the Egyptian gods, cults and symbols were received in classical times. Numerous monographs have been written on the Oriental cults (generally implying those of Egyptian origin) and their introduction into and influence on the world of Greece and Rome. Despite various vicissitudes under some of the Roman emperors the Egyptian cults enjoyed worship and reverence far beyond Mediterranean shores, and in many instances continued to exert various influences down to the Renaissance and even later. Erik Iversen, in his book *The Myth of Egypt and its Hieroglyphs in the European Tradition* (Copenhagen, 1961, p. 9), notes how 'the melting-pot of Neo-Platonism transformed the waning memories of ancient Egypt into a living mythos, which from the time of the Renaissance became an inexhaustible source of inspiration to European artists and mystics, and to men of letters and scientists as well'. Such was still the power, influence and effect of the gods and symbols of ancient Egypt several millennia after their first appearance in the Nile valley.

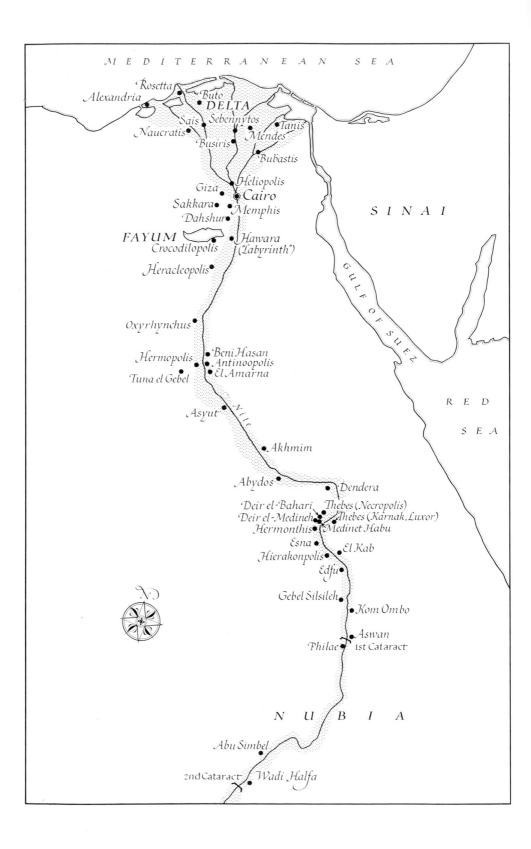

MEDITERRANEAN SEA

Rosetta

Alexandria

Buto

DELTA

Sais

Sebennytos

Tanis

Naucratis

Mendes

Busiris

Bubastis

Heliopolis

Giza

Cairo

Sakkara

Memphis

Dahshur

FAYUM

Hawara
("Labyrinth")

Crocodilopolis

Heracleopolis

SINAI

GULF OF SUEZ

Oxyrhynchus

Hermopolis

Beni Hasan

Antinoopolis

El Amarna

Tuna el Gebel

Asyut

Nile

Akhmim

RED

SEA

Abydos

Dendera

Deir el-Bahari

Thebes (Necropolis)

Deir el-Medineh

Thebes (Karnak, Luxor)

Hermonthis

Medinet Habu

Esna

El Kab

Hierakonpolis

Edfu

Gebel Silsileh

N

Kom Ombo

Aswan

Philae

1st Cataract

NUBIA

Abu Simbel

2nd Cataract

Wadi Halfa

The Dictionary

IMPORTANT NOTE

*Where references are made in translations of original
texts in the following entries, those from the Pyramid
Texts follow the enumeration of section-numbers of
the hieroglyphic texts as in Faulkner, 1969 (not the
numbers of Utterances). Chapters from the Book of
the Dead follow the sequence of 'Spells' given in
Allen, 1974.*

A

A bronze **Aegis** with the head of the goddess Isis wearing a crown of uraei and flanked by two falcon heads representing Horus. From Sakkara, Late Period. Petrie Collection, University College London.

The scribe Ani worshipping **Aker**, represented as two lions back to back with the symbol of the horizon between them. Book of the Dead of Ani, XIX Dynasty, *c.* 1250 BC. British Museum.

Acacia The gods were supposed to have been born under the sacred acacia of the goddess Saosis, north of Heliopolis. According to one Pyramid Text (No. 436) Horus emerged from the acacia. Later traditions linked the tree not only with birth but also with death. In the Book of the Dead (Chap. 125) the deceased is led to the acacia by children. According to the ritual of the Coffin Texts portions of the sacred acacia of Saosis are squashed and bruised by the deceased. A supernatural healing effect was attributed to these portions.

Aegis The imprecise term 'aegis' refers to a collar-like necklace which was regarded as a symbol of protection. In the Book of the Dead there is a spell for the 'collar of gold which is placed around the neck of the transfigured spirit on the day of burial'. These collars are often decorated with the head of a falcon or a uraeus. The placing in position of the collar is a symbolic expression for being encompassed by the arms of the god. In the temple of Seti I at Abydos there is a representation in the chapel of Re-Herakhty in which the king presents a collar with a pectoral attached for the clothing of the divine image. This rite is part of the morning office at which the priest says, 'O Atum, you place your arms around Re-Herakhty that he might live together with his ka in eternity!'

Collars with animals heads, (i.e. divine symbols) above them also adorn the prow and stern of divine barques. Jewellery collars with the head of a god or goddess are also called an aegis. On the lids of mummy cases and stone sarcophagi instead of a collar there can appear a representation of a vulture with outstretched wings which has the same meaning; the sarcophagus of Tuthmosis I is an example.

Air Air was personified by the mythical figure of Shu who separated Geb, the earth, and Nut, the sky, who were locked in embrace. Air became a symbol of life, hence the fact that one text of the Herakleopolitan Period says of Shu that 'his name is life'. It was related concerning the Theban god Amun that he was 'the breath of life for everyone'. Without air one could not breathe and without breath there was no life. The 'Book of Breathings', a composition of the Late Period, was said to have been written by Isis for her dead husband Osiris 'to animate his soul'. In order to breathe air in the netherworld, i.e. to survive after death, the deceased had to identify himself with Shu 'who in the realms of the gods of light draws upon the air of the celestial lakes. His effectiveness reaches unto the limits of heaven.... May the air refresh the young god, the awakening one, with healing power.'

Aker The god Aker embodies the earth. He is represented as a narrow tract of land with a human or a lion head at either end, or simply in the form of two lions seated back to back. One animal faces to the west where the sun sets and begins its journey into the night, where the realm of the dead is situated; the other animal faces the east where the sun rises every morning from the realm of darkness. Pictures show Aker bearing the barque of the sun, thus symbolizing the nightly journey of the sun through Aker's kingdom. The two lions or lion-heads guard the entrance and exit to the underworld. In the Pyramid Texts it is said of the men to whom the gates of the underworld are opened, 'the gates of the earth-god (Aker) are opened unto you' (Nos. 796; 1014; 1713).

Amulet These small figures were hung round the neck or placed with the deceased in the tomb and were meant to protect the wearer. Several formulae are known from the Book of the Dead which, when recited, endow the amulet with magical powers. The most important forms of amulets are divine figures (e.g. Osiris, Bes, Taweret), animal figures (e.g. lion, ram, scarab), parts of the human body (wedjat-eye, hand), royal insignia (especially crowns) and actual symbols such as the ankh and djed pillar.

The head-rest, a protection against the loss of the head, is worthy of special mention. In the Book of the Dead (Chap. 166) it is said of the deceased 'Doves awake thee from sleep.... They alert thee to the horizon. Raise thyself .... Ptah has overthrown thy enemies.... Thou art Horus, the son of Hathor ... to whom a head was given after it was cut off. Thy head cannot be taken from thee hereafter; thy head can never be taken from thee'.

Amun Amun, together with his wife Amaunet, is mentioned in the Pyramid Texts (No. 446) as a primeval god, but after the

Silver statuette with details in gold of **Amun** wearing his characteristic head-dress of a crown surmounted by a disc and tall plumes. New Kingdom. British Museum.

Eleventh Dynasty he seems to appear as god of Thebes. The Egyptians interpreted his name as 'the hidden one', for he was the effective force in the invisible wind. Also, because of a derivation from the Libyo-Berber language 'aman', i.e. water, it is believed that Amun as primeval creator god was chiefly worshipped as a goose. Generally the ram with curved horns is regarded as his sacred animal, a reference to his aspect as a god of fertility (ithyphallic representations of him as Amun-Min also indicated this). A further animal manifestation is that of a snake in which the god bears the name of Kematef, 'he who has completed his time'. As god of the Theban capital Amun attained the position of supreme State god in the New Kingdom, and as Amun-Re was identified with the sun-god. Lastly, the god 'he who abides in all things', was imagined as the soul (*ba*) of all phenomena.

Anat She was a Syrian goddess introduced into Egypt at a later date. Like her male counterpart, Reshef, she had a warlike nature and was represented as a woman carrying a shield and an axe.

Anhur *see* ONURIS

Animal Animal cults may have been motivated first of all by man's fear of animals and their usefulness. Animals became media of revelation and also the bearers of supernatural powers and archetypal qualities, hence the fact that the bull symbolized the power of generation and the cow motherliness. It is possible that various ancient Egyptian nome gods had their roots in the theriomorphic patron deities of prehistoric chieftains. In all localities there were sacred animals protected by taboo that were regarded as the manifestations of gods. Only rarely was the god regarded as the animal itself, except, for example, in times of religious decline. The individual animal was only an earthly image of the transcendent primeval image, the theriomorphic form of which expressed some particular aspect of a divine entity. Sacred animals were, therefore, the 'eternal soul' (as the ethnologist Frazer described it) or, as the Egyptians would say, the *ba* of the gods. The ram was the soul of Amun-Re, the Apis bull that of Ptah, and the crocodile was the *ba* of Suchos.

As the divine image became anthropomorphized in historic times, only the animal head was retained in many instances. At the end of the New Kingdom animal cults gained precedence. Individuals of a sacred species, which were recognizable by special markings, were enthroned in the temple at their individual cult centres. Not only these but also free-ranging members of the sacred species were mummified after death and interred according to prescribed formulae.

Some animals were especially revered at one or more cult centres. There was the cat at Bubastis; the ram at Mendes, Herakleopolis, Esna and Elephantine; the bull at Heliopolis (Mnevis bull), Memphis (Apis), and Hermonthis (Buchis); the cow at Dendera and Aphroditopolis; the crocodile at Kom Ombo and Crocodilopolis; the ibis at Hermopolis and Abydos; and the falcon at Edfu and Philae. In the vast underground galleries discovered at Sakkara there are literally thousands of mummies of ibises, hawks and baboons. The quality of the mummified animal provided for the devotee to offer varied considerably, obviously depending on the amount that the devotee would pay.

Animal sacrifice Sacrifice was based on the idea of nourishment. Gods and dead persons only sated themselves upon the 'essence' of the offering, therefore the material could be offered to several recipients until it was finally eaten by a priest. The sacrificed animal was regarded as a symbolic embodiment of the god's enemy. When a bull was sacrificed in honour of Osiris the following spell was recited: 'I hit him who is in the form of a bull who hit you.' The sacrificial animal was, therefore, equated with Seth. The most usual sacrificial animals were geese, goats, cattle and antelopes, the latter of which were especially close to the divine opponent, Seth, because their mutual home was the desert. The animals were inspected for purity before the sacrifice and were then festively adorned. After the animal had been slaughtered by severing the jugular vein it was dissected with a flint knife.

Animal skins Animal skins were an important requisite for one's outward appearance when one wished to achieve a final inner transformation, therefore a skin was a symbol of a transitional state. Three fox skins were used as the written sign for birth. Bes, the protective god of childbirth began by wearing a lion skin on his back and later a panther skin on his breast. The notion of rebirth was presumably connected with the skin under which lay the Tekenu, the substitute figure of the deceased. The so-called *sem*-priest who officiated at the 'Opening of the Mouth' ceremony which was important for survival after death wore a panther skin as his official garb. Several Old Kingdom sarcophagi show a panther skin in relief on the lid.

Ankh The original meaning of the ankh is still debatable. Gardiner suggests it was a sandal-strap, or it may be a magic knot. The hieroglyphic sign means 'life' (*'nḫ*) and as a symbol it points to divine, i.e. eternal, existence. Therefore it is a recurrent attribute of the gods who hand it to the king. Air and water were the vital elements, for which reason they can be circumscribed by the use of the ankh, as when a god holds the ankh before the king's nose, giving him the 'breath of life', or when streams of water in the form of ankhs run over the king during ritual purification. As a symbol of an imperishable vital force the ankh was used on temple walls, stelae and elsewhere; it is particularly evident in friezes of objects usually in the region of the feet, hence the fact that people saw in it the image of a sandal-strap. This sign, also called the *crux ansata*, entered the symbolism of the Coptic Church because of its cruciform shape.

Anointing Various oils were used from the earliest times for the usual anointing employed to care for the body. Seven types were mostly mentioned. Anointing then entered cult as a symbol of purification. The divine image was not only washed but also anointed. In one hymn to Amun it says, 'Oil and wax are mixed with myrrh in order to boil the unguent intended for your limbs'. The deceased also needed unguent, for purification and transfiguration. Because of its fragrance unguent acquired a further significance, i.e. to smell sweetly like a god meant thereby to share in divine grace. The deceased were depicted many times raising a vessel of oil to their nose. The god Horhekenu, i.e. 'Horus of unguent', who was venerated in Bubastis also bore the epithet 'lord of protection', a metaphor for the protective power of unguent.

Antelope A white antelope was the ancient sign for the sixteenth Upper Egyptian nome. Originally, the goddess Satis, the 'Lady of Elephantine' who dispensed the cool water of the cataract, was probably venerated in the form of an antelope, hence in historical times her head-dress consisted of the Upper Egyptian royal crown and two curved antelope horns. There was a connec-

The goddess Hathor offers the **Ankh**, symbol of life, to the pharaoh Amenhetep II. She wears her characteristic head-dress of cow's horns and sun disc and a uraeus on her forehead. The king wears the nemes head-dress and uraeus. Above his head his name and titles are given as 'Son of the Sun, Amenhetep, given life for eternity'; Hathor has her name and titles above her head. Tomb of Amenhetep II (1450–1425 BC), no. 35 in the Valley of the Kings, Thebes.

tion between the antelope and water in symbolic reasoning, therefore the gazelle, a type of antelope, was sacred to the other cataract goddess, Anukis.

In Southern Arabia the antelope was the symbol of the god Attar who brought the country's rain. In Egypt the antelope suffered the fate of most desert animals, for since they belonged to Seth they were outlawed and persecuted. The sign of the sixteenth Upper Egyptian nome at a later date, therefore, shows the Horus falcon triumphant over the antelope.

Anubis The god of the dead and of embalming with the epithets 'lord of the hallowed land', i.e. the necropolis, and 'he who is before the divine booth', in which mummification took place. He usually had canine form, although the species, whether dog or jackal, cannot be exactly identified. Anubis guarded the mummy from evil forces in the night. The image of a recumbent black jackal was included on the doors of numerous rock tombs for he was the guardian god. When the body was embalmed a priest wearing a jackal mask acted as Anubis' representative. After the rise of the cult of Osiris, Anubis became subject to the new ruler of the dead. He then conducted the 'Weighing of the heart' in the Hall of Judgement before Osiris and the 42 gods.

Anuket *see* GAZELLE

Anukis (Anqet) A goddess of the region of the First Cataract at Aswan, and one of the triad of Elephantine. She was the wife of the god Khnum and mother of Satis. Representations generally show her as a woman holding a tall papyrus sceptre and wearing a high crown of feathers. There was a temple dedicated to her on the island of Seheil in the Cataract, and she was especially worshipped to the south in Nubia.

Ape In the Archaic Period there was a baboon god called 'the great white one' (Hedj-wer), who was in the Pyramid Age already regarded as a form of the god Thoth. The latter was the patron of scribes, inventor of hieroglyphs and lord of the divine writings. There are several representations in which his sacred animals sits on the back of the head or shoulders of the scribe, keeping watch over him. Seated apes above the outlets of water clocks also symbolize Thoth as god of chronology. Originally Thoth may have been a god of the moon, and sculptures or rep-

Painting of **Anubis** embalming the deceased, laid out on a bier, in the tomb of Nekhtamun, a *wab* priest of the cult of Amenhetep I, 'Chancellor of Amun, Servant in the Place of Truth'. At the left hand end of the bier stands Isis, and at the right, Nephthys. Both goddesses pour water, lustrating the mummy from tall vases. Isis is also shown kneeling with outstretched wings, her throne hieroglyph upon her head, above the scene. The walls of the chamber are entirely covered with scenes of Nekhtamun with various gods and goddesses. On the left can be seen the goddess Maat, and the god Ptah standing in a kiosk. XIX Dynasty, 1320–1200 BC. Tomb no. 335, Deir el-Medineh, Thebes.

resentations of baboons often bear the moon-disc on their heads. Even better known is the relationship of apes to the sun. The screeching of apes at daybreak was interpreted as an act of homage. In pictorial representations the rising sun is therefore greeted by baboons with forepaws upraised. Often obelisks, as emblems of the sun, have a series of baboons in this stance sculptured around their pedestal base. Two giant sculptures of baboons in quartzite, squatting on their haunches, are at Hermopolis, the site sacred to Thoth.

Apis Apis was the most important among the sacred bulls of the Land of the Nile. Originally a fertility symbol; other attributes were later added. Because his cult centre was in Memphis he came into contact with the god of that city, Ptah, becoming his herald and, finally, Ptah's 'glorious soul' which appeared on earth in the form of a bull. After his death Apis was assimilated into the god Osiris, hence one speaks of Osiris-Apis, hellenized as Serapis. Apis himself became a mortuary god. After the Late Period he was represented on many coffins as a sacred bull running with the mummy of the deceased to the tomb. After the New Kingdom he bore the sun-disk on his head.

Upon his death the Apis was buried with great ceremony in the vast underground galleries of the Serapeum at Sakkara, the cemetery of Memphis. These were discovered by Auguste Mariette in 1851, and the tomb of the cow mothers of the Apis-bulls, the Iseum, were discovered in 1970 by W. B. Emery.

Apophis Each morning and evening the serpent demon threatened the sun-god and thus endangered world stability. The 'huge serpent' was the embodiment of the opponent of God and a symbol of the powers of darkness. Therefore Apophis was equated with Seth, the enemy of the gods. Each morning, when the sun emerged from the netherworld, and each evening at the beginning of its nightly voyage, the sun barque was attacked by the serpent. This caused the sky to be dyed red with the blood of the defeated and wounded Apophis. The serpent also tried to hinder the sun's journey with its coils, described as 'sandbanks'. Several extant ritual texts refer to the 'overthrowing of Apophis' and provided magical protection, of which it was written 'it really saves him (i.e. the protected person) from all evil'.

Architecture *see* GROUND PLAN; PYRAMID; TEMPLE

Bronze figure of an **Apis** bull showing all his special markings, as described by Herodotus, and wearing the disc and uraeus on his head. Dedicated by Peteesi. XXVI Dynasty, *c.* 600 BC. British Museum.

Relief of Akhenaten, Nefertiti and three of their daughters in a touching scene. The disc of the **Aten** above sends its rays down towards them, ending in small hands which hold the ankh sign of life to the nostrils of the king and queen. XVIII Dynasty, c. 1370 BC. Staatliche Museum, Berlin.

Arrow   The bow and arrow is one of mankind's most ancient weapons and often a divine attribute in the myths of the ancient orient. The arrow as a symbol of divine power was personified in Neith, whose cult symbol consisted of two crossed arrows. Two crossed arrows on a shield were the emblem of the fourth and fifth Upper Egyptian nomes which were the true regions of Neith worship. Two crossed arrows were also representative of the power of the hemsut, the female counterpart of the *ka*. Lastly, the bow and two arrows, together with the spear and club, were the weapons of the patroness of Thebes, Waset. Arrows could also symbolize the sun's rays: Atum was the archer who sent out his shooting beams like arrows, and in a list from the Graeco-Roman period which recorded the forms of the daytime sun, the seventh hour was represented by a monkey shooting arrows. When the king shot an arrow to each of the four cardinal points at his accession this was supposed to symbolize the fact that his might reached to the ends of the earth.

Arsaphes   The name which Plutarch has handed down as Arsaphes refers to the Egyptian Herishef, i.e. 'he who is upon his lake', a primitive fertility god in the form of a ram. Herishef 'on his lake', the primeval waters, appeared in Herakleopolis as an 'image' of the sun god. In the Ninth and Tenth Dynasties he was identified with Re and received the solar disc as a head-dress. Since he was also equated with Osiris he could wear the Atef crown as well. The fact that Herishef was praised as a giver of sustenance and that he walked at the head of gods bringing offerings can be traced back to his original function as a fertility god. There is also a probable connection between his title 'lord of awe' and the ram's head which served as a symbol for worship and respectful fear. According to Greek interpretation the god was assimilated with Herakles.

Ass   In the speech of the Egyptians the word 'ass' was a metaphor for a tormented beast of burden. In the other world there were ass-headed demons who guarded the gates of the underworld. With few exceptions the ass was an opponent of divine powers. Seventy-seven asses stood in the way of the sun in order to prevent the sunrise. Already in the Middle Kingdom the animals which bore the corn were regarded as Sethian entities who carried off Osiris who was present in it. Once Seth had been outlawed his animal became a scapegoat. After the

New Kingdom the festival of Osiris included a rite in which the 'ass of Seth' was stabbed with a spear. In Busiris it was sufficient to use a loaf of bread stamped with the image of an ass as a symbolic offering. The hieroglyph for 'ass' bore two knives stuck between the shoulder blades in order to render the animal's typhonic power harmless.

Astarte A very popular goddess in the Near East of Syrian origin. She was introduced into Egypt in the Eighteenth Dynasty where she was seen as a goddess of war and regarded as a daughter of Re, or alternatively of Ptah. Generally she is represented as a naked woman riding bareback on a horse wearing the atef-crown and brandishing weapons. She often appears sketched on the small limestone flakes (ostraka) that workmen in the necropolis doodled on.

Atef *see* CROWNS

Aten To begin with, Aten signified the sun as a heavenly body. Later the visible disc of the sun was seen as a manifestation of Re. It is said of the sun god that 'his body is Aten'. Under Tuthmosis IV Aten is referred to on a large commemorative scarab and the sun was already being personified; Aten was the sun disc itself. Amenhetep IV, who changed his name to Akhenaten ('incarnation of the Aten'), exalted Aten to the position of sole god and demythologized his image. In the first five years of his reign Aten was still being represented as a human being with a falcon's head, like the Heliopolitan Re-Herakhty, but after that there was only the sun disc whose arms ended in hands holding the ankh.

Atum The creator god of Heliopolis is a figure for speculation. He was a personification of the primeval chaos from which issued all that exists. He was 'he who came into being of himself'; before heaven and earth were separated he was the 'Lord of all'. In the Pyramid Texts (No. 199) he appears as the primeval hill and he was also thought to be present in the image of the scarab, who seems to emerge from a ball of earth. The great granite scarab of Amenhotep III by the sacred lake at Karnak was dedicated to Atum. The serpent as a chthonic animal could also be a manifestation of the god. In the Book of the Dead (Chap. 175), Atum addresses Osiris concerning the end of the world and announces that he will destroy all he has made and turn himself back into the primeval serpent.

Atum begat by copulating with himself (Pyramid Text No. 1248); one must avoid using the word masturbation, which is offensive and incorrect in terms of Egyptian mythology. Thus he produced the first divine pair, Shu, the air and Tefnut, moisture (No. 1249). The hand which he used to copulate with himself was personified as the female principle inherent in him. 'Atum and his hand' appear as a divine couple on coffins of the Herakleopolitan period.

B

Ba Horapollo translated the word 'ba' as 'psyche', but it had very little similarity to the classical conception of the soul. The *ba* was a psychic force. In the earliest religious texts anonymous gods were simply described as *ba*. Then the word became employed as a synonym for the manifestation of a god. Thus people saw the *ba* of the sun-god Re in the phoenix of Heliopolis, and the Memphite Apis was worshipped as the *ba* of Osiris. There are also places, however, where one god was the manifestation of another, as when Osiris was called the 'soul of Re'. In connection with the king the concept *ba* referred to his authoritative, indeed his divine power.

At the end of the Old Kingdom the term *ba* was applied to all people. Then it became the possessor of imperishable powers. Tomb paintings and papyri of the New Kingdom show the *ba* in bird-form hovering above the mummy of the deceased or sitting on the trees planted round the tomb. Mortuary spells, being magically effective, were supposed to make it possible for the soul to 'assume any forms it wishes'.

Barque The barques used for cult purposes corresponded to a large extent to Nile boats. Where the cabin normally stood there was a naos with the god's image. Prow and stern were adorned with the head of the god or his sacred animal, often surmounting a jewelled collar, an aegis. The barque was normally carried in procession on the shoulders of priests. The barque of Osiris, called Neshmet, was famous. The god went out in it at the beginning of his ceremonial drama in order then to return like one who

Bronze figure of the cat goddess **Bastet**. She holds her aegis in her left hand and a Hathor-headed sistrum in her right. At her feet are four small kittens. Late Period. British Museum.

The sedge and the **Bee**, symbols of Upper and Lower Egypt, as part of the titles of Senusret I (1971–1928 BC) carved on his processional kiosk in the temple of Amun at Karnak. Middle Kingdom, XII Dynasty.

has awakened from the dead. The Egyptians wished to take part in the journey of the Neshmet after death, and thereby to participate with Osiris in resurrection. Elsewhere the conception of the passing over of the dead was linked with the image of the sun barque. *See also* SOLAR BARQUE.

Bastet This goddess was especially worshipped at Bubastis and had in early times already been grouped with Tefnut and Sekhmet. From an inscription of Ramesses IV we know that it was forbidden to hunt lions on the festival of Bastet. The goddess was regarded as the mother of the 'savage-faced' lion-god Miysis who bore the epithet 'lord of slaughter'. With the Middle Kingdom the cat appeared as Bastet's sacred animal and after the New Kingdom she was depicted with the cat's head. The goddess' character became more and more friendly. She was connected with the moon and in myth became the eye of the moon. The 'raging' aspect of earlier times was transferred to the goddess Sekhmet, who thereby became the negative, destructive side of Bastet.

Bee An aetiological myth tells that the sun-god Re once wept and his tears fell to earth, changing themselves into bees. Honey had a certain importance in the manufacture of unguents. A very early scene of beekeeping occurs on a relief from the Fifth Dynasty sanctuary of Re at Abu Gurob. Lower Egyptian kings of the Predynastic and Early Dynastic Period had the epithet 'he who belongs to the bee'. In contrast, the Upper Egyptian rulers were called 'he who belongs to the sedge'. Bee and sedge then became part of the royal titulary in the ensuing period. The temple of Neith in the Delta town of Sais was named 'house of the bee'.

Benben *see* OBELISK

Bes The deformed figure of Bes with his mask-like face was regarded as a protective spirit who averted evil. His name included several dwarf-like spirits, all with deformed legs and the face of a cheeky and good-natured old man, often with his tongue hanging out. Originally these entities wore on their backs a lion skin, of which only the ears and tail remained. In later times, after the late New Kingdom, Bes often wore a panther skin, with the head and claws across his breast. In the Eighteenth Dynasty pictures of a winged Bes were popular. His most important attributes were the *sa*, symbol of protection, a knife for defence, and musical instruments whose sound scared off evil spirits. A special form of Bes was called Aha, i.e. 'fighter', who is seen throttling two serpents with his bare hands or seizing hold of a Sethian gazelle. Bes was supposed to ward off evil spirits. His image was worked into head-rests, beds, mirrors and cosmetic pots, the latter because unguents and cosmetics served to avert the evil eye, as well as being for beauty care. He is especially represented in Mammisi, the subsidiary buildings of temples in the Late Period, in which the annual mysteries of the birth of the divine son were celebrated, as in the 'birth house' at Dendera on the roof of the temple.

Birth brick Two bricks were often used as footrests for women when squatting to give birth. These so-called birth bricks were believed to determine one's destiny. According to the Rhind Papyrus, Thoth carved the time of one's death into them. The birth stone was personified by the goddess Meshkhent, and whilst the child was yet in the womb she fashioned its *ka* and announced its destiny at birth. In the circle of Abydine gods, four Meshkhents appear as servants of Isis. Besides anthropomorphic depictions the goddess was also shown in the form of a birth brick with a woman's head attached. *See also* KHNUM; KING.

Bisexuality The primeval gods appeared in many myths as bisexual; they impregnated and they also gave birth. Bisexuality was a symbol for the absolute nature of the creator who was confined to no one sex and who needed no partner. Therefore, Atum produced Shu and Tefnut for himself. Horapollo relates that the Memphite demiurge Ptah was regarded as both male and female. Representations of the Late Period often show the god with female breasts. The Nile-god Hapi is also shown as a bisexual being with a beard and the pendant breasts of an old nurse. The Theban goddess Mut was the 'mother of him who begat her' — a linguistic symbol of her all-embracing motherhood which necessarily included fatherhood. One representation even shows her with a phallus. The goddess Neith 'created the seed of gods and men' and bore the epithet 'father of fathers and mother of mothers'. At Esna the creator god Khnum could also be addressed as Neith; thus she represents the female counterpart present in him.

According to a papyrus in the Louvre, Paris (No. 3079), Isis says of herself in the

Figure of the grotesque dwarf-god **Bes**, carved in sandstone within the temenos of the temple at Dendera. Ptolemaic Period, after 116 BC.

Carving of women seated on **Birth** stools beside a relief of surgical instruments. Ptolemaic Period, after 203 BC. Temple of Kom Ombo.

play concerning the tale of Osiris' death, 'I turned myself into a man, although I was a woman in order to make your [i.e. Osiris'] name endure on earth'. The ancient Egyptian did not see it as unnatural that the gods should possess the sexual potency of both sexes. Even the child of Horus, Imsety, was given androgynous features otherwise he could not have been represented in the Middle Kingdom as a beardless man with the yellow skin colour of a woman.

Black To be precise black is not a colour at all but an absence of colour. It denoted the netherworld, the ruler of which, Osiris, was often called 'the black one'. The patron goddess of the Theban necropolis, Queen Ahmes-Nefertari, was predominately shown with a black skin, although she was not of Nubian or negroid descent. The mortuary gods, Anubis and Khenti-Amentiu, were depicted as recumbent dogs or jackals with jet-black coats. The black god was 'lord of the white land'. In one representation in the temple of Deir el-Bahari the god of the dead promises Queen Hatshepsut long life. Images of Min, the god of fertility and especially of generation, were painted with a mixture of fine resin and carbon dust in accordance with ancient ritual. *See also* COLOUR.

Block statue *see* CUBE STATUE

Blood Creative power was attributed to the 'effluxes' of deities. A myth tells how Hu and Sia came into being from the drops of blood which fell when Re was circumcised. The cedar grew from the blood of Geb, the earth god, and two persea treas sprouted from the drops of blood of Bata in the Tale of the Two Brothers. It is uncertain as to how far the knot of Isis (the tet), which is addressed in the Book of the Dead as 'O blood of Isis', was connected with the concept of blood as a lifegiver. The idea that this may bear some connection to the menstrual blood of the goddess is probably not wholly erroneous. *See also* ISIS, BLOOD OF ISIS.

Board game In origin the board game was probably a symbolic reference to the battle between the two cosmic powers. An echo of this is to be found in a tale which Plutarch related. According to this the sky goddess Nut was caught by her husband being unfaithful in marriage, so he cursed her so that she could only give birth on days which were not on the calendar. Nut therefore turned to intelligent Thoth who went to the moon god and in a board game won from him a seventieth part of each day to make five new days out of them on which Nut could give birth. In the New Kingdom the magical meaning took predecence. Board games were placed with the dead in the tomb to secure an afterlife. On winning the game, the squares on the board being linked to divinities, one inferred that the journey to the other side would have a happy conclusion. Representations of the deceased seated playing a board game (generally alone) occur in tombs (e.g. that of Queen Nefertari in the Valley of the Queens), and as a vignette in copies of the Book of the Dead.

Book of the Dead A funerary text that was usually written on papyrus (occasionally on leather) placed with the burial of those people sufficiently wealthy to be able to afford a copy. The quality and length of the copy varied in relation to the owners' standing and provision for his or her burial. The Book of the Dead consists of a number of Chapters, or 'Spells' (Allen, 1974, lists 174 Chapters), aimed at the protection of the deceased in the netherworld. The text is found written in hieroglyphic, hieratic and demotic script and the best copies are embellished with vignettes at the heads of the Chapters and various scenes throughout. The most popular scenes represented are the Ceremony of the Opening of the Mouth and the Weighing of the Heart in the Hall of Judgement before Osiris. Amongst the finest extant papyrus copies for private persons are those of Ani and Hunefer (Nineteenth Dynasty), and the best royal examples are those of Queen Nodjmet and the princess Nesitanebashru (Twenty-first Dynasty); both these came originally from the great cache of royal mummies officially discovered in 1881 at Deir el-Bahari. All four papyri are in the British Museum, London.

The Book of the Dead stands at the culmination of a long line of funerary texts that begin with the Pyramid Texts in the Fifth Dynasty and graduate through the Coffin Texts of the Middle Kingdom until they reach their fullest form as the Book of the Dead at the beginning of the New Kingdom. The number of Chapters in any one copy of the Book of the Dead varies, as does their content and the selection of the Chapters to be included by their individual owners. There are several versions of the texts, the best known and most common is that of the Theban recension. Some Chapters are better known than others, and are common to most copies, notably Chapter 6, the Ushabti Chapter, 'for making a ushabti work for a man in the God's domain', and Chapter 30, the Heart Chapter, 'for not letting N's heart oppose him in the God's domain'. Many of the protective spells seem rather extreme, but they were all viewed as most necessary precautions to ensure the well-being of the deceased in the next world.

Bow The image of the nine bows, which symbolized the Pharaoh's subject peoples, originated in the earliest historical period. The national goddess of Upper Egypt, Nekhbet, bore the epithet 'she who binds the nine bows', an indication of the unification of several peoples of tribes under the authority of the king. In the mortuary temple of Senusret I at Lisht the triumph of the king over his enemies is illustrated by the fact that he stands on nine bows. The bow is an attribute which characterizes the war goddess, Neith.

Bread Bread brought to the altar was blessed by priests and was then regarded as sacred bread. Presenting an offering could bring one into direct contact with a god for on a statue from Deir el-Bahari the inscription reads, 'lay cakes before me that I may speak to Hathor'. The central position of bread as an offering is shown on one papyrus according to which sacred loaves were found in the pupil of the eye of Horus, which was a generalized symbol for offerings.

Bread was important among grave gods; it was found in the tomb of Tutankhamun as an offering of natural produce. In the Book of the Dead (Chap. 52) the text states, 'I live on these seven loaves of her whose loaves have been brought by Horus and by Thoth'. The deceased hungers for the bread of life when he beseeches Re, 'I come to you; be merciful, countenance of Re . . . give me bread for I am hungry'. Represented at the bottom on the offering table were often round or oval loaves or possibly cakes.

Buchis The sacred bull of Hermonthis (Armant) south of Thebes. He was regarded as an incarnation of Re and Osiris. Like his counterpart at Memphis, the sacred Apis bull, Buchis was buried in great splendour in a vast underground catacomb called the Bucheum. This was discovered, ravaged throughout the centuries, by Robert Mond and W. B. Emery in 1927.

Bull In the Archaic Period the bull was already thought of as having a special rela-

The scribe Ani playing a **Board game** accompanied by his wife Tutu. Book of the Dead of Ani, XIX Dynasty, c. 1250 BC. British Museum.

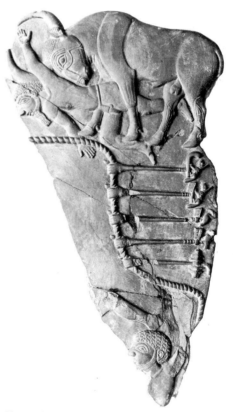

Slate palette showing a mighty **Bull**, representing the pharaoh goring an enemy. He stands above standards representing five of the nomes of Egypt hauling on a rope, probably attached to captives. A similar scene appears on the Narmer palette. From Hierakonpolis, c. 3100 BC. Louvre Museum, Paris.

Numerous **Bulls' heads** modelled in clay but with real horns were found decorating a low bench in front of the 'palace façade' of the tomb of king Djet, or Uadji, no. 3504, excavated at Sakkara. I Dynasty, *c.* 3000 BC.

tionship to heaven. One Pyramid Text (No. 470) mentions the 'Bull of Re who has four horns' which guarded the roads of heaven. The sun and moon bore the epithet 'bull of heaven'. The symbolic significance of this animal found expression in the bull cults which were spread throughout the land. The Lower Egyptian nomes had a bull as their emblem. The sacred Mnevis bull was regarded as a mediator of the god, Atum; the Apis was the 'glorious soul' of Ptah, and Buchis, who was venerated in Hermonthis (Armant), was regarded as the 'living image of Month', but was also seen as the herald of Re.

As the great inseminator the bull was imbued with the power of life and conveyed the water of life. The personification of the cosmic waters, Nun, was given a bull's head to distinguish him. The inundation, so important for the fertility of the land, could appear in the image of a bull, whilst a later term for the flooding was simply 'gift of the bull'. The ithyphallic gods, Min and Atum, were called Kamutef, i.e. 'bull of his mother'. The kings of the New Kingdom often bore the epithet 'mighty bull' or 'strong bull of Horus', whilst in the Archaic Period the ruler was regularly depicted as a bull, as on the Narmer palette where the king pushes down the wall of a town with his horns and throws its protector to the ground with his hooves. *See also* APIS; BUCHIS; MNEVIS.

Bulls' heads In the Predynastic and Archaic periods the custom prevailed of decorating sacred buildings and altars with the skulls of sacrificed bulls or antelopes. These bulls' heads were probably a device to avert evil forces. In historic times the skulls of sacrificed animals were only present in isolated cases among which one may mention the bulls' heads on poles at the entrance to the tomb of Ramesses III. The cult symbol of Hathor, 'bat with the two faces', originally had two bovine heads instead of human ones. The Hathor column can be traced back to this fetish set on a pole.

Burial The actual burial was preceded by the funeral ceremonies. The necropolis usually lay to the west of settlements because that was the place of the setting, and therefore dying, sun. As the mummified corpse crossed the Nile two women symbolically played the parts of the goddesses Isis and Nephthys who bewailed Osiris. Great significance was attached to the journey of the deceased over the water. A 'journey over

Reconstruction of a Predynastic **Burial**. The corpse is crouched on its left side, surrounded by food offerings to sustain him on his long journey into the next world. Before 3100 BC. British Museum.

the lake' was already known from the Old Kingdom, and in the Late Period mummies, or models of them, were floated on water on the back of a crocodile, the latter being an allusion to the rescue of the dead Osiris by Horus who appeared as a crocodile. The crossing in a Nile boat was supposed to be reminiscent of the divine barque and there are plays on the idea of the solar barque, for example, in the Book of the Dead, Chap. 67, where it says 'I embark on my throne in the barque of Re. May I not be distressed through being left boatless on my throne in the great barque of Re'. Even when transported over land the coffin rested on a bier which lay on a sledge pulled by oxen or cows. Before the mummiform coffin was lowered into the tomb it was stood upright and the ceremony of the Opening of the Mouth was performed. The belief in a possible afterlife, not unlike earthly existence, led to the practice of placing all the necessities of life in the tomb with the deceased. Wine jugs and milk bowls have been found, but they had not been hollowed out, which was obviously meant to signify that they would always remain full. Little models of ships, houses, granaries, workshops, etc., were also placed there. Reliefs and paintings on the tomb walls were not so much to inform survivors about the life of the dead, but rather to perpetuate the life which had been extinguished, and to serve as a magical power, thus prolonging for eternity the deceased person's enjoyment of his earthly possessions. *See also* TOMB.

C

Canopic jars They were four in number and intended to receive the wrapped viscera removed from the body of the deceased during the embalming process. The earliest evidence of evisceration in ancient Egypt comes from the calcite canopic chest, divided into four compartments, found at Giza in the tomb of Queen Hetepheres, the mother of Khufu (Cheops) of the Fourth Dynasty. Each canopic jar (or compartment in a divided chest) held a particular organ of the body and was under the especial protection of one of the Four Sons of Horus. Each had a characteristic head and was associated with

Set of limestone **Canopic jars** of the princess Neskhons. Each carries the appropriate text on it for the geni (one of the Four Sons of Horus) that protects the internal organs enclosed in the jar. From left to right they are: Hapi (ape), the lungs; Duamutef (jackal), the stomach; Imsety (man), the liver; and Qebsennuef (falcon), the intestine. From Deir el-Bahari. XXI Dynasty, *c.* 1000 BC. British Museum.

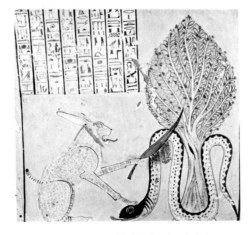

Painting in the tomb of Inkherka showing the great **Cat** cutting off the head of the serpent Apophis entwined around the persea tree. XX Dynasty. Tomb no. 359, Deir el-Medineh, Thebes.

one of the four cardinal points of the compass and one of the four 'protective' goddesses. After the New Kingdom the following arrangement became established:

Imsety – man-headed – held the liver – south – Isis

Hapi – ape-headed – held the lungs – north – Nephthys

Duamutef – jackal-headed – held the stomach – east – Neith

Qebsennuef – falcon-headed – held the intestine – west – Selket

During the Eighteenth Dynasty the stoppers were sometimes all human-headed. Tutankhamun's stoppers were portraits of him wearing the nemes headcloth. They plugged the four compartments of his canopic chest, each of which held a miniature gold coffin containing the viscera and inscribed with the prayers due to the relevant son of Horus. The four protective goddesses were sculptured at each corner on the outside of the chest. In the Late Period the viscera was bandaged and returned to the body cavity and often a dummy set of canopic jars was provided for the burial.

The Greeks gave the name of Canopus, the legendary hero, pilot of Menelaus, to a port on the Mediterranean coast near Alexandria. The god Osiris was worshipped there in the form of a jar with a human head of the god. This representation of the 'Canopus of Osiris' also appeared on some of the coins struck under the Roman emperors at the mint of Alexandria. From this human-headed jar early Egyptologists gave a common generic name of 'Canopic jar' to all and any such vessels of pottery or stone with human-head-shaped stoppers that came from Egypt. The name therefore has no origins in antiquity, it arose from a misconception and has now entered Egyptological parlance.

Cartouche The apotropaic power of the ring served to protect the king. The ruler's two most important names were surrounded by the cartouche. These two names were the throne name (prenomen), which designated him as king of Upper and Lower Egypt, and the birth name (nomen) which was introduced by the title 'son of Re'. The expansion of the name led to a longer form. The rope was a symbol for 'that which the sun's disc encircles', i.e. the universe, therefore the cartouche could also allude to the Pharaoh's authority over the world. From the Eighteenth Dynasty various royal sarcophagi imitated the shape of the cartouche (e.g. Tuthmosis III), a fact which also suggests that it signified power and might. Even on the rectangular sarcophagi of Tuthmosis I and Hatshepsut there was an encircling cartouche clearly engraved on the lid. *See also* SEREKH.

Cat The archetypal image of the 'great cat who dwells in Heliopolis' probably did not refer to the domestic cat, but to the short-tailed jungle cat which lived in the thickets of the Delta, for there is no reference to the domestic cat until the Eleventh Dynasty. Because it was hostile to snakes it became a sacred animal of the sun god. It is related in the Book of the Dead (Chap. 17, and often illustrated) that the 'great cat' cuts off the head of the Apophis serpent whose body threatens the sacred persea tree. In the New Kingdom the male cat was regarded as an incarnation of the sun-god and the she-cat was equated with the solar eye. Feline figures may display a scarab, the symbol of the rising sun, engraved on the head or breast thus showing their solar significance. The domestic cat attained special significances as the sacred animal of Bastet. Hundreds of figures of cats were set up as votive offerings in the temple at Bubastis in order that the donor might share in the goddess' grace. Actual mummies of cats were buried in their thousands in special cemeteries in the area.

Cavern The cavern was closely associated with the 'great mother' archetype. The female image of the hollow space was the seat of birth and death. The necropolis area of Lycopolis bore the name 'cavern mouth'. The life-giving waters of the Nile issued from a cavern which was linked in the Pyramid Texts (1551) with the 'hall of justice', the place where the Osirian court of the dead sat. The Nile god, Hapi, dwelt in a cave, guarded by snakes under the granite rocks of the First Cataract at Aswan. Occasionally Hapi took the place of Osiris. In the book of the nether-world, Amduat, the sixth hour of the night was called 'body of Osiris', i.e. the nadir of the sun's daily journey, whilst the seventh hour, called 'cavern of Osiris', alluded to the turning point. In the twelfth hour the sun god, Re, still had to crawl through the body of a snake 1300 cubits long, an image of a narrow cave mouth, and was reborn in the form of Khepri.

Censing Censing firstly had a purificatory purpose, for incense 'cleanses and adorns'; it also freed one from typhonic forces. Incense itself was regarded as a supernatural manifestation and was termed 'the sweat of the god, which fell to earth'. In the mortuary cult the rising smoke of incense was seen as a signpost to the other side. Temple reliefs often show the presentation of the 'divine fragrance'. A bowl was used as a censer which after the New Kingdom stood at the end of a holder shaped like a human arm, whilst the other end terminated in the head of a deity. A second bowl was used to hold the grains of incense, and these were dropped onto the glowing charcoal in the bowl at the end of the holder.

Centipede In the Pyramid Texts (No. 244), it states that 'The serpent is in the sky, the centipede of Horus is on earth'. The minor god Sepa, whose name means 'centipede', was worshipped in Heliopolis. He was evoked as a charm against noxious animals and enemies of the gods. In accordance with the centipede's chthonic nature Sepa was connected with the necropolis and was equated with Osiris as a mortuary god.

Centre The Egyptians, like the Babylonians and Assyrians, believed their land to be in the centre of the earth. According to the Leiden Hymn to Amun, Thebes had 'come into being before any other city', for it was from there that the first men originated, who then founded all other cities. Mention must be made of the primeval hill of the Heliopolitan cosmogony which arose from the waters of the beginning and was a special symbol for the centre. Other politically important towns, above all Memphis, laid claim to this notion. As the town of the creator god Khnum, Esna became the 'divine hill, the top of which emerged from Nun'. Egypt was conceived to be the centre of the earth, since the world had begun there. In order to proclaim his accession to all the world the ruler had four birds released towards the cardinal points. It is certain that the image of the universe as represented on a sarcophagus of the fourth century BC (Metropolitan Museum, New York) goes back further in time. The sky goddess bends over the earth, here represented as a disc uplifted by the *ka* sign. The outer surrounding ring may be regarded as the ocean, the next ring between the goddesses of east and west represents the foreign lands and, lastly, in the third ring are the forty-two standards of the Egyptian nomes. Horapollo in the fourth century AD was still well aware that Egypt was the centre of the inhabited world, just as the pupil is the centre of the eye.

In contrast to the nations of the ancient orient the concept of the universal tree, or Tree of Life, was less apparent. According to the Heliopolitan tradition, as on the Metternich stela, the sun flew up in the form of a bird at the beginning of the world and alighted on the primeval tree, the willow. Both the palm and obelisk, as manifestations of the sun god, could come to signify the axis of the world.

Child Since the child is near to the beginning of existence it bears the power for future beginnings. It was itself a symbol of development, of becoming. The 'Child Horus', whom the Greeks called Harpocrates, enjoyed special veneration among the Egyptians. In fact he embraced all youthful gods who were worshipped under the name of Horus as solar or primeval deities. There are figures of Harpocrates as a sun-child sitting on the lotus flower. The childish gesture with the finger upon the mouth, typical of Egyptian representations, was interpreted by the classical world as a symbol of silence. Harpocrates could also coalesce with the figure of Nefertum who was likewise worshipped as a young sun-god. As a symbol of beginning the child is found in lists of the Graeco-Roman Period as a form of the first and second hours, whilst the tenth to twelfth hours show an adult deity with a partially stooped back supporting himself on a stick.

The king was regarded as a son of Osiris, called Harsiese, who was actually the son of Isis conceived by her through the dead Osiris. Khnum formed the divine child and his *ka* on a potter's wheel. From the day of the accession it was hoped that the expectations of the miraculous birth would be fulfilled, that the world, threatened by chaos, would be rejuvenated by the childlike forces which were close to the origin of things and therefore unused. The 'divine child', wearing the Upper Egyptian crown, became the symbol for a Delta nome (*see* p. 89, Nos. 18 and 19), later splitting into an upper and a lower nome. Connections with a primitive worship of the child Horus are possible but have not been proved.

Children of Horus *see* HORUS

Cippus of Horus *see* HORUS

An effigy of Osiris wrapped in linen winding sheets was found in a box in the 'Treasury' of the tomb of Tutankhamun. When unwrapped it revealed a hollow frame in the figure of the god which had been filled with Nile mud and seed to make a germinating Osiris, or **Corn mummy**. From the tomb of Tutankhamun (1362–1351 BC), no. 62 in the Valley of the Kings, Thebes. Egyptian Museum, Cairo.

Coffins *see* SARCOPHAGUS, COFFIN

Colour To the Egyptians the word 'colour' meant the same as 'substance', of which colour was not an accidental but an integral part. When it was said of the gods that one could not know their colour it meant that their substance was inscrutable. In painting an emotive aspect was attributed to colour apart from its function of covering surfaces. Therefore red, the aggressive, life-giving, and at once threatening, colour was placed in juxtaposition to blue which is subdued and yet flows out into infinity. Amun's blue coloration alluded to his cosmic aspect. Other gods wore blue wigs or beards. Ambivalent concepts of colour were displayed especially with regard to black which was a reference to death and the netherworld but, at the same time, to rebirth. Colour also distinguished one thing from another as in the case of the russet-coloured men against the pale yellow women. The early Fourth Dynasty statues of Rahotep and Nofret were already painted in this way.

Red and white were also opposites. When placed in juxtaposition to each other, they were an expression of wholeness and perfection. The White Crown of Upper Egypt and the Red Crown of Lower Egypt were worn by a single ruler of all Egypt in the form of the Double Crown. Bread made from white grain and beer from red were food and drink in the netherworld. In the case of hippopotami, the 'red' male animal and the 'white' female animal were distinguished, the former being outlawed as hostile and the latter regarded as sacred and helpful. *See also* BLACK; GREEN; RED; WHITE.

Column Other nations of the ancient Near East held the widespread, symbolic concept that temples and palaces were models of the structure of the cosmos, therefore columns became a type of support for heaven. The palm column belonged to the sphere of concepts concerning the view that the sky was a palm in the spreading crown of which the sun-god appeared. The papyrus columns of the New Kingdom with their closed or open flower capitals represented the path of the sun-god, for papyrus plants are closed at sunrise and unfurl in the light. Both types of capitals are found in the temple complex of Luxor and in the mortuary temple of Ramesses II at Thebes. Columns also had a symbolic function apart from their architectural purpose. In the Hall of Annals of Tuthmosis III at Karnak the entablature was supported by two columns which still stand today; one shows the heraldic plant of Lower Egypt, the papyrus, and the other the Upper Egyptian heraldic plant, the lotus. The hypostyle hall of the Ptolemaic temple at Dendera has twenty-four columns surmounted on all four sides by the head of Hathor (*see* p. 58).

Corn, corn mummy, Osiris bed Corn, from which was made not only bread but also beer, was a general symbol for life-preserving forces, rather than of life itself. This is one reason why representations in tombs of the cultivation of corn exceeded all other scenes in number. The personification of corn was Nepri, whom the Coffin Texts called 'one who lives, having perished', thus alluding to the seed-time and the harvest. The power of Osiris, the god of vegetation, was displayed in the sprouting of the seed. When the seeds were trodden in by goats or pigs this was regarded as the victory of Seth over his brother, and the sprouting corn was a symbol of Osiris springing back to life. There are representations, especially in the papyri, which show the young shoots sprouting from the body of the dead Osiris, whilst the god himself lies on a bed composed of five ankhs and ten *was*-sceptres. During the god's mysteries an image of the dead deity was fashioned in mud and sown with grain. Such germinating corn mummies were supposed to manifest the unconquerable nature of life and, when placed with the deceased in the tomb, were a magical aid to continued existence.

Cosmography *see* LADDER OF HEAVEN; SUPPORTERS OF HEAVEN

Cow The cow was seen as the sacred animal of the goddesses Hathor and Isis. The sacred animals of Hathor were called Zentet-cows and the nomarchs of Dendera in ancient time bore the title 'herdsman of the Zentet cow'. The goddess of heaven Hathor was herself worshipped in the form of a cow. In the Book of the Dead (Chap. 148) seven cows and their bull were invoked in order to provide sustenance for the transfigured dead. The 'great wild cow' was regarded as mother of the king who was often compared to a wild bull. In the myth of the divine birth of the king the Hesat-cow suckled the young king; the Hesat was also supposed to be mother of the mortuary god, Anubis and the Apis bull. As an animal which was connected to heaven and also to the netherworld the cow became a

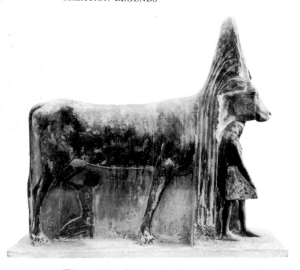

The goddess Hathor as the sacred **Cow** with the pharaoh Amenhetep II drinking from her udder. From the Hathor shrine at Deir el-Bahari. XVIII Dynasty, c. 1440 BC. Egyptian Museum, Cairo.

Small bronze statuette of the **Cow**-headed Isis, mother of the sacred Apis bull. On her head is an ornate crown of plumes, cow horns and disc above the royal uraei. The inscription around the base is a dedication by the donor of the figure. From Sakkara. Late Period. Petrie Collection, University College London.

symbol of the hope for a continued existence. The beds on which the coffin rested during the obsequies had the form of a cow's body. During the Osirian mysteries the god's body was laid in a wooden box of bovine form, that he might be reborn from the womb of the celestial cow.

The burial place, the Iseum, of the sacred cows that were the mothers of the Apis bull was discovered at Sakkara in 1970, not far from the Serapeum, by W. B. Emery.

Creation legends There are several creation legends in ancient Egyptian religious literature, and they tend to become rather confusing. It is not possible to say which was the most widely accepted of them since this varied according to the place which had promulgated the legend, its political influence at any given time and the religious climate of individual periods. Several of the legends are concerned in one way or another with a mound rising above the primeval flood waters, or with a supreme god who was self-engendered.

In the tradition from Heliopolis, the centre of the early sun cult, a mound emerged from the watery chaos Nun with Atum upon it who begat himself and then went on to create the god Shu (air) and the goddess Tefnut (moisture). They in turn gave birth to the earth god Geb and his sister the sky goddess Nut. Shu, their father, separated them by lifting up Nut into her place in the sky – a scene often represented in various papyrus copies of the Book of the Dead.

At Memphis the creator god Ptah conceived the idea of creation in his heart and it was given effect by his tongue which spoke the thought. Creation by utterance occurs in numerous of the texts.

Hermopolis had two traditions. One told of a primordial mound that rose above the primeval waters. It was given a gift by the creator god (in this instance Thoth) of an egg which opened and gave birth to a young sun that immediately rose up into the heavens. Thereafter followed at long intervals the rest of the creation of all living things. The second Hermopolitan tradition still used the primeval waters but this time a lotus bud floated on its surface. The petals opened to reveal the young infant sun, Horus on the primeval flower, and his beneficent rays spread over the world. The basic element of the primeval mound is reflected in the architecture and planning of some temples where there is a gradual rise in the floor level from the entrance towards the naos in the sanctuary, which on its elevation represents the primeval mound. It is a feature readily apparent in sectional drawings of temples, especially in the temple of Horus at Edfu.

The essential element that is common to all the Egyptian creation legends is that the creation proceeded in stages, balanced and orderly, the very embodiment of the concept of stability implied by the word *ma'at* which governed all things (except when it broke down in the Intermediate Periods).

Crocodile There were several crocodile cult centres throughout Egypt. At Athribis in Lower Egypt the crocodile-god Khenty-Khet was worshipped and he quickly assumed the form and nature of the falcon god, Horus. In the Fayum and in the vicinity of Thebes temples were built to the crocodile god Suchos. At Kom Ombo there was a large crocodile necropolis. The dreadful strength of the crocodile induced not only fascination but awe. Horus, as the avenger of his father, and the divine hunter appears on the walls of the Ptolemaic temple at Edfu slaying with his spear the animal that was regarded as Seth's henchman, and therefore an enemy to the gods. Also at Edfu, during the great festival of Horus, two clay figures of crocodiles were cursed and destroyed. Dendera probably venerated the crocodile in the Archaic Period since the nome sign was composed of such an animal. Later the feather adorning the head was interpreted as a symbol of Osiris and the whole nome sign was explained as the victory of Osiris over the crocodile, the embodiment of Seth. In the underworld the deceased were threatened by a crocodile. The seventh hour of Amduat was guarded by a huge crocodile of whom it was said, 'whoever knows this is one whose *ka* the crocodile does not devour'. In this connection one must bear in mind the crocodile-headed monster in the Hall of Judgement who was called the 'devourer of hearts'. Lastly, the earth-god Geb could also appear in the form of a crocodile in the Book of the Dead. The beast's dangerous gaping mouth was an expressive image of the abyss. *See also* SUCHOS.

Crook The crook, *ḥkȝ* in Egyptian, was a sceptre which was not only carried by gods and kings but also by high officials. The more ancient, almost man-high crook was once a shepherd's staff and was still found later as an attribute of the shepherd god Anedjti. Out

Most frequent of the scenes represented from **Creation legends** is that showing the air god Shu separating the sky goddess Nut from the earth god Geb. He is assisted here by two ram-headed gods described in the text beside them as 'souls'. The owner of the papyrus, the princess Nesitaneba-shru, is shown kneeling in adoration at the bottom right and also in the register above as her own soul, as a *ba* bird, between two walking rams. From Deir el-Bahari. Book of the Dead of Nesitanebashru, XXI Dynasty, *c.* 1000 BC. British Museum.

Granite statue of Ramesses II (1304–1237 BC) showing him carrying the **Crook** and flail, symbols of royal authority, crossed on his chest. He wears a short wig held by a diadem with the uraeus at the front and above it the Double Crown of Upper and Lower Egypt. From Elephantine. XIX Dynasty. British Museum.

The **Crowns** worn by the pharaoh had special significance. Top to bottom are: the White Crown (*hedjet*) of Upper Egypt; the Red Crown (*deshret*) of Lower Egypt; the Double Crown (*pschent*) of the Two Lands; the Atef Crown; and the Blue or War Crown (*khepresh*).

of this grew the well-known, smaller form with a more pronounced hook. In the written script this sceptre meant 'to rule'. In the Middle Kingdom the staff was placed in friezes on coffins as a symbol of Osiris.

Crowns The insignia of gods and kings also had symbolic significance. Crowns alluded to the character of their wearers; they were above all a symbol of power. According to an ancient inscription the crown nourished the king in order that he might share in its power. As rulers of the 'Two Lands' kings wore the Double Crown, called the *pschent*, which was a combination of the mitre-like crown of Upper Egypt, the White, and the Red Crown of Lower Egypt. These two crowns were thought to embody the protective goddesses of royalty, the Upper Egyptian Nekhbet and the Lower Egyptian Wadjet. Since the time of Snefru the crown of double feathers, consisting of two upright ostrich plumes, was worn by the king. From the Eighteenth Dynasty the ruler wore the blue Khepresh crown with round gold adornments, the so-called war helmet. The Atef crown, worn predominantly by Osiris, was a combination of the crown of double plumes and the Upper Egyptian crown, but unlike this it had a small solar disc on the tip instead of the blunted peak. The Egyptian who tended to syncretism saw the crowns as the eye of the sun-god but also as the uraeus and as flame protecting the king.

Cube statue The cube or block statue was a block of stone in the form of a squatting figure. The purpose was not that stone and figure should be as one but rather that they should remain mutually independent. This design which first appeared in the Middle Kingdom was not only an imitation of a squatting man but was also a symbolic expression of the hope of resurrection. The stone block embraced the deceased like a womb, for the posture alluded to the foetal position. Westendorf described the cube statue as a symbolic form of the mother goddess, Isis. The strong, plain surfaces of the Middle Kingdom statues were covered all over with inscriptions in the New Kingdom examples, almost as if the sculptors of the later period were driven by a *horror vacui*.

D

Dance Among all peoples dance was probably of sacred origin. According to the Roman author Lucian the Egyptians liked to express the secrets of their religion in dance. During the processions of Min dancers appeared as the god. At the 'festival of drunkenness' the king danced in the form of Shu in front of Hathor in order to 'expel her anger'; to the goddess dance was the 'food of the heart'. In the mortuary cult dance became a symbol of the hope of resurrection. Muu dancers wearing reed crowns ran 'at the door of the tomb' towards the deceased, who was equated with Osiris, and greeted him with shouts of joy.

Darkness Impenetrable darkness, along with water, is one of the primeval realities. According to a Ptolemaic text Kek was the god of darkness, the first being to assume a form out of the amorphous gloom. With the emergence of light, which appeared as the sun on the primeval hill or as a sun-child from the lotus flower, the ordered, created world became visible, but the latter had to battle with the chaotic forces of darkness who were hostile to the gods and to life. The sphere of Pharaohs' influence stretched as far as the 'region of primeval darkness', as texts of the New Kingdom often state. The enemy of the sun, Apophis, lived in darkness. In the tenth hour of Amduat the sun-god enjoined his warriors with the words 'may your arrows be swift, your spears sharp and your bows strung that you may punish my enemies who dwell in the darkness outside the horizon'. The damned had always to remain in eternal darkness; as the Book of Caverns states, 'they see not the rays of the sun-god neither do they hear his voice; they are in darkness'. As a ruler of the netherworld Osiris also dwelt in darkness which he, like the blessed dead, hoped to overcome.

Deification Unlike the Greeks the idea of deification of mere men was not widespread amongst the Egyptians. There was a basic concept that the pharaoh was the living Horus on earth who became Osiris upon his death, but he was already a god born on earth and so was not, as such, deified by his translation at death. There are a few instances where men were deified and ranked with the gods, some of them being relatively obscure viziers of the Old Kingdom. The best known is Imhotep, the architect of the Step Pyramid at Sakkara and vizier of the pharaoh Zoser in the Third Dynasty. Imhotep was deified some two thousand years after his death when he became a god of medicine, wisdom and learning, identified with Aesculapius by the Greeks. Stelae and offerings to him have been found in great quantities at Sakkara. Also an architect, Amenhetep-son-of Hapu, the confidant of Amenhetep III of the Eighteenth Dynasty, became a god of healing with a small cult shrine at Deir el-Bahari.

The idea that drowning in the Nile led to deification was popular in the Late Period. It is well illustrated by the two brothers Pedesi and Pehor who were drowned in Nubia and became the focus of an important local cult. They were worshipped in a small temple at Dendur, and may have been actually buried in a concealed chamber that lay behind the centre of the stela in the sanctuary. This temple has now been removed and reconstructed in the Metropolitan Museum of Art in New York. Even more famous in Roman times was Antinous, the favourite of the emperor Hadrian (AD 117–138). He was drowned in the Nile, some would say sacrificed, and a city, Antinoopolis, founded at the spot where his body was recovered.

Demons Demons were a force to be reckoned with in ancient Egypt, but they were not so prevalent there as in many of the other early civilizations of the ancient Near East. A number of the Chapters in the Book of the Dead are aimed at thwarting demons and preventing them carrying off or harming various parts of the body of the deceased. Demons were the messengers of the goddess Sekhmet as the embodiment of evil, and they did her bidding in spreading disease and pestilence. One of the most feared was the 'Eater of Hearts', an obnoxious creature part crocodile, part lion, part hippopotamus, that is represented crouching beside the scales upon which the heart of the deceased is being weighed in the ceremony of the Weighing of the Heart in the Hall of Judgement scene in the Book of the Dead.

The later tombs in the Valley of the Kings, especially those of Ramesses VI and IX, have many demons featured in the paintings on the walls, and they also appear in bright colours on the walls of tombs of some of the princes buried in the Valley of the Queens, e.g. Khaemweset, a son of Ramesses III. Although demons are, by implication, evil there were good demons who acted as protectors and guardians, generally of ways of entry, and of the coffin in its tomb.

Demotic Demotic script is, literally, the 'popular' script. It originated under the Twenty-sixth Dynasty (700–600 BC) and was the only form of script generally and widely used for the next thousand years. It reflected the popular language, and was much favoured for government and legal documents. The centre band of inscription on the Rosetta Stone is in demotic. Although the origins of demotic lie in business hieratic script, it is far more developed; it has its own grammatical structure, a vocabulary that is new, and many additional signs, abbreviations, and ligatured letters. It is very much more difficult to read than either hieroglyphs or hieratic.

Desert The Egyptians associated the idea of desert with barren land, quarries, uplands, cemeteries and all non-Egyptian areas, everything, in fact, which lay outside the fertile, black earth of the Nile valley. People believed that the endless desert to the west of the Nile valley was the entrance to the underworld in which the rebirth of the sun and of the deceased was accomplished. Depictions in books of the netherworld show the realm of the dead as surrounded by a broad strip of sand. Wasteland was described in this way in the 'Book of the Caverns'; it was called 'great sand'. In the eleventh hour of Amduat four goddesses are designated as powers of punishment by the sign for 'desert' on their heads. Their names are: 'she who cooks', 'she who provides heat', 'she who is upon her sand', and 'destroyer'. The god of the western desert, Ha, was represented in human form and wore the sign for desert as an attribute on his head. Seth appeared in mythology as the 'red' god, representative of the hostile desert and continued, therefore, to become the adversary of Osiris, the god of vegetation.

Deshret *see* CROWNS

Dismemberment Finds from several predynastic and earlier dynastic graves seem to indicate that the bodies were dismembered, but closer investigation has shown this to be questionable; mostly it is a case of secondary damage as, for example, when grave robbers disturbed the body, especially after it was reduced to a skeleton. The latter consisted of removing the perishable flesh from the bones, a measure which served the purposes of funerary beliefs.

The myth of Osiris displays a true dismemberment motif. The tearing of the lunar god into fourteen pieces alluded to the fourteen days of the waning moon. The last crescent was, therefore, regarded as the leg. Among ancient peoples the growth of plants was connected with the phases of the moon. Dismemberment was a prerequisite for the reawakening of the dead or for the sprouting of vegetation from his corpse. Pictures show new seed growing from the dead body of the god of vegetation. It has not yet been clarified as to whether there is any connection between Osiris and the bull called 'the dismembered one' (*ḥsb*) who was venerated in the eleventh Lower Egyptian nome. Plutarch equated Osiris with the Greek god Dionysos, who was called Zagrus in his bovine form and was torn into pieces by the Titans.

Divine staff Divine staves were poles decorated with the heads of certain deities or their sacred animals, but in contrast to the standards the divine images did not stand on a transverse beam. These staves, kept in the inner sanctuary and carried in procession, were not only regarded as a mere attribute but as a manifestation of the deities' godhead. The staff of Amun, identified by the ram's head with uraeus, which was taken on campaigns, was supposed to place the ruler under divine protection. On his Libyan campaign Ramesses III took the holy staff of Amun with him in his own chariot. Horus was 'lord of the staff in order to make a way for him'. His staff, with which the god hunted the hippopotamus of Seth, was often shaped like a harpoon. Several representations are known from the New Kingdom in which priests and officials hold divine staves in their hands. *See also* STANDARDS.

Djed, Djed-pillar The djed-pillar is a prehistoric fetish, the meaning of which has still not been unequivocally explained. It may be a stylized representation of a leafless tree or a pole with notches in it. The most probable interpretation is that the djed was originally a pole around which ears of corn were tied in tiers. The pillar played a role in rustic fertility rites, for it was a symbol of power in which the energy of the grain was preserved. Over and above this it became a general symbol of 'stability' and as such entered the written language. In the Old Kingdom at Memphis there were some priests of the 'noble djed', and the chief Memphite god, Ptah, was himself called 'noble djed'. The ritual of 'raising the djed pillar' began at Memphis; the king himself performed it by means of ropes and with the assistance of priests. This symbolic act referred to the hoped-for stability of the monarchy.

Once Ptah had been equated with Sokar, the god of the necropolis, and the latter with Osiris, the erstwhile fetish became a symbol of Osiris at the beginning of the New Kingdom. Therefore the djed was regarded as the god's backbone. Coffins of the New Kingdom often have a djed-pillar painted on the bottom where the backbone of the deceased would have lain, thus identifying him with Osiris. Besides the previously mentioned meaning, the raising of the djed-pillar symbolized the victory of Osiris over his opponent Seth who had 'laid the djed on its side'. Because it merged with the symbolism of the beyond the djed became a most meaningful piece of funerary jewellery.

Door The threshold of a door was a barrier and likewise a crossing point. The door was a dual symbol for defence and entry. Figures of lions were often placed at the entrance to temples or the bolts were given leonine features in order to protect the temples from typhonic forces. Gates played a special role in the journey of the deceased through the next world. There was actually a 'Book of the Gates', which has come down to us without its original title and which described the path of the sun-god through the netherworld where doors guarded by fire-spitting serpents and other demons had to be breached. There is a fine representation of the twelfth division of the netherworld in the tomb of Amenhetep II in the Valley of the Kings. Symbolic significance was certainly also attributed to the doors of temples and those leading to tomb chambers. Inscriptions in most pyramids (i.e. those of the Fifth and Sixth Dynasties) in the access corridor between the ante-chamber and the tomb-chamber allude to a 'high gate' which was often described as the 'gate of Nut', i.e. the gate of heaven. The opening of the shrine doors during ritual were the symbolic opening of the gates of heaven.

Wall relief in the temple of Seti I at Abydos showing Seti raising the **Djed**-pillar, i.e. resurrecting the god Osiris, with the assistance of Isis. *Top:* The djed-pillar alone, holding the crook and flail, was a substitute symbol for Osiris. XIX Dynasty, *c.* 1310 BC.

Double *see* KA

Duality The Egyptians experienced duality less as two contrasting elements but rather as two complementary ones. Awareness of duality is nothing more than a further development of unity; that which the westerner sees as contrasting symbolism was complementary symbolism to the Egyptian. One of the finest examples is the image of the solar barque. The boat was really the crescent moon which carried the sun-disc. The close connection of the sun and moon is also apparent in the case of the Apis bull, between whose horns (symbol of the crescent moon) the sun-disc rested, which is similar to the head-dresses of the goddesses Hathor and Isis. Just as Osiris and Isis belonged together on the mythological plane so did men and women in the earthly realm; and the battle between Horus and Seth corresponded to the counterbalance of light and darkness. Heaven and earth were not opposites but together they constituted the complete world just as the 'Two Lands' in their unity constituted Egypt. According to the principle of duality gods themselves were divided into representatives of Upper and Lower Egypt, therefore the Nile god and the goddess of cultic song, Meret, were characterized from time to time by wearing on their heads the heraldic plants of Lower Egypt (the papyrus) and Upper Egypt (the lotus) respectively. The realm of the dead, called Amenti and Duat, and paradise, called Sekhet-Hetep and Sekhet-Iaru also had dualistic aspects.

Duamutef *see* CANOPIC JARS

E

Ear The ear referred symbolically to the readiness of the mind to be receptive to that which it had heard. Ears represented in holy places were a sign that prayers were heard and they therefore alluded to the goodwill of the gods. Many stelae showed images of huge ears; these were thought to be a magical pledge that the prayer would be brought before the gods.

Edjo *see* WADJET

Egg The egg played an important part in conceptions of the beginning of the world because life issues from it. According to

ancient myth the first god came into being from an egg which had lain in a marsh thicket. In the Book of the Dead the text speaks of the 'hidden' egg of the 'great cackler'. It is not clear to which god this referred, but it was possibly Geb or Amun. According to another reference in the Book of the Dead (Chap. 77), the sun-god himself emerged from the egg as a falcon and already in the Coffin Texts of the Middle Kingdom part of the spell ran 'O Re who is in his egg'. Ptah was addressed as the creator of the egg. Representations show the god fashioning the egg on the potter's wheel. Oviform amulets were popular through which a man hoped to possess the power of the demiurge residing in them. Such amulets were also placed with the deceased in the tomb. The term 'egg' which denoted the inner coffin next to the mummy was particularly significant because it implied hope of an afterlife.

Ennead of Heliopolis This was the earliest group of nine gods, *pesedjet*, which other cult centres later copied. The nine gods, the Great Ennead of Heliopolis, were: Atum, the creator; his children Shu and Tefnut; their children Geb and Nut, and then the brother and sister quartet of Osiris and Isis, Set and Nephthys. *See also* CREATION LEGENDS; NUMBERS; OGDOAD.

Eye As the organ which takes in light, colour and images the eye became one of the most important symbols in ancient Egypt. It often appears as an amulet in the form of the wedjat-eye. In the Pyramid Texts (1266) two 'evil eyes' are mentioned which seal the door-catch. Even the Egyptians were aware that the eyes shone, beamed, flashed and glowed and these aspects therefore became tokens of authority and a symbol of fire. The uraeus was regarded as the fire-spitting eye of the sun-god. The sun and moon were the eyes of the god Horus of whom it was written, 'when he opens his eyes he fills the universe with light but when he shuts them darkness comes into being'. The name of Osiris means 'place of the eye' for his name in hieroglyphs has represented an eye above a throne. Until the Eighteenth Dynasty it was common to adorn the left-hand side of a coffin with a pair of eyes so that the deceased might see his way through heaven. At the end of the New Kingdom and in the Saite Period the eye is found on mummy cases, also in the area of the breast or feet, but now with amuletic significance representing rather the eyes of Horus, which were offered to the deceased.

Various Egyptological researchers like to trace Egyptian representations of the eye back to the eye of the falcon god, Horus. A more recent piece of work points, on the other hand, to the bull's eye, the edge of which was outlined with black and green eyepaint along the nasal bone and lower eyelid. The unity of the green lower lid and the white iris actually symbolized the unity of the Green (or Red) Crown of Lower Egypt and the White Crown of Upper Egypt. Lastly, the eye was also equated with the barque: 'your right eye is the evening barque and your left eye is the morning barque'.

Eye of Horus *see* HORUS

Eye of the Moon *see* MOON

F

Falcon The soaring flight and aggression of the falcon gave him a special position in cult. In the Pyramid Age the image of the falcon already served in the written language as a general determinative for god. As king of the air the falcon became the sacred animal of the king of the gods, Horus, and also a symbol of divine kingship. Falcon statues wearing the double crown, as the large granite example in the temple of Horus at Edfu, are to be understood in this way. Horus was a sky god who protected the earth with his wings. There were other falcon gods besides him: Month, the god of war who wore a crown of tall double plumes, the sun-god Re who bore the sun-disc on his head, and the mortuary god, Sokar. Hathor was often characterized as a female falcon in equation with Horus as sky god. In the Pyramid Age the ascension of the king was represented as the flight of a falcon. The *ba*-bird, symbol of the soul, was also usually depicted in the form of a falcon. In the Late Period mummiform coffins, or the mummies themselves, often had a falcon mask, as the silver coffin of the pharaoh Sheshonq II from Tanis, in the Cairo Museum.

False door An offering niche was set into tombs and mortuary temples. The back of the niche was shaped like a false door, a symbol for the relationship between the living and the dead. The *ka* of the deceased was supposed to be able to leave the tomb in

Gold head of a **Falcon** with a tall, plumed head-dress that formed part of a composite statue. The body was probably of wood, to which the head was attached with copper nails. The bright, beady eyes are the polished ends of a rod of obsidian (volcanic glass) passed through the hollow head. From Hierakonpolis. V Dynasty, *c.* 2400 BC. Egyptian Museum, Cairo.

The spirit of the dead, the *ka*, was thought to be able to pass through the **False door** to partake of the offerings left by the priests of the mortuary cult on an altar in front of it. Often the owner is shown seated before a table piled with food, and here, beneath him, is inscribed long lists of various kinds of food and the quantities required for offering. From North Sakkara. Mastaba tomb of Khaubau-Sokar. Late III Dynasty, *c*. 2630 BC. Egyptian Museum, Cairo.

this way. The image of the dead person was often placed on the surface of the door, in order to make this purpose more obvious. In the New Kingdom rock tombs of Thebes false doors were no longer in relief, but only painted on. The decoration in the window-like area above the false door showed the deceased before an offering table.

Field, arable land As the produce of the fields represent offerings to the gods, so the field itself can become a symbol for an offering. Ramesses III numbered among his merits the fact that he increased the lands of the temple of Re-Herakhty 'in order to double the divine offerings in great abundance for your mighty, honourable and beloved name'. A stele of King Tefnakht (Twenty-third Dynasty) shows the king presenting the sign for 'field' (a basket with three reeds) to the goddess Neith of Sais and to the god Atum. It is evident from the inscription that the 'offering of the field' is linked to the hope that the gods will grant the king (eternal) life.

According to the Osirian beliefs regarding the hereafter the deceased must work in the fields of Iaru, 'the field of reeds', in addition to fulfilling other functions which had been his during his lifetime. The ploughing, sowing and harvesting as represented in the illustrations in the Book of the Dead are an expression of the hope for an afterlife. The growth of the barley and spelt (Book of the Dead, Chap. 109), which attain supernatural height in paradise, is one of the conceptions of the abode of the blessed.

Fire The religious significance of fire was founded upon human experience of its destructive and yet beneficial power. This all-consuming element was embodied in the uraeus, the fire-spitting eye of the sun-god. One myth called the home and birthplace of the sun-god the 'isle of fire', which was certainly a metaphor for the dawn, from which the daily light of the sun breaks.

The flame was regarded as a symbol of purity and purification, for it drove off the power of Seth and annihilated evil. Among the attributes of Taweret, the hippopotamus goddess, one finds a torch, the flame of which was supposed to exorcize dangerous demons. In the Late Period torches were often burnt in order to cleanse the deceased from earthly defilement.

The uncanny, destructive power of fire played a great role in conceptions of the other world according to the Coffin Texts. Fiery rivers and fire-spitting entities threatened survival after death and are very reminiscent of the medieval Christian vision of hell. On the other hand, the dead person was able to overcome the demonic powers of this apocalyptic hereafter if he could change himself into a shooting flame. In the fifty-ninth scene from the Book of the Gates the damned were exposed defenceless to the fiery breath of the huge serpent Amemet who had already appeared in Amduat as a fire-spitting snake. Gods with the sign for fire on their heads or on their wings consumed the enemies of the sun-god. In the fifth hour of Amduat red, wavy lines denoted the 'lake of fire', the heat of which destroyed the damned but whose water refreshed the blessed dead.

Fish The fish was generally regarded as an unclean animal. Hallowed personages like the king, priests and the transfigured dead were not allowed to receive them as food. When the Osirian beliefs spread, fish became identified with the evil Seth. According to a tradition stated by Plutarch, the people believed that the lepidotus fish (Nile carp), oxyrhinchus fish (mormyrus) and the phagrus fish (perhaps a type of bream) had together eaten the phallus of the dismembered Osiris. On certain feast days therefore fish, as typhonic animals, were burnt and trampled underfoot as an offering to the gods.

On the other hand, fishes were regarded as sacred animals. In Mendes the goddess Hatmehit was venerated as the 'first of fishes'. The fish she wears on her head may be a dolphin. The latus or Nile perch was sacred to Neith. The oxyrhinchus fish received special honour for despite the above-mentioned tradition it was an Osirian animal which was supposed to have come into being from the god's wounds. This fish was also associated with Hathor at Esna and occasionally examples are represented with the Hathor crown. Fish were also associated with the sun for the chromis, with its reddish fins, and the lapis lazuli blue abdu, or Abydos fish, escorted the solar barque and warned of the approach of the hostile serpent.

Flabellum The flabellum had symbolic value besides its being a practical means of giving shade and creating an air-current. It was a medium for obtaining divine power and is often found in pictorial representations behind divine animals. The flabellum was a cult symbol of the god Min and it also symbolized a man's shadow, to which it alluded when in conjunction with the *ba*-bird.

The labour in the **Fields** of the hereafter is often represented in the tombs of the nobles of the New Kingdom and in the funerary papyri. In every instance there is an abundance of water shown, and crops that stand higher than a man. The deceased did not seem to mind having to work in the fields but was not prepared to assist in the corvée of shifting sand and clearing the irrigation canals, for which purpose ushabti figures were provided in quantity with the burial. Book of the Dead of the priestess Anhai, XX Dynasty, *c.* 1100 BC. British Museum.

Flail The so-called flail (*nḥȝḥȝ* in Egyptian) consisted of a short rod with two or three pendant strips or strings of beads. It is often considered to be a shepherd's whip, which was exalted to a symbol of authority through its connection with the god Anedjti, the 'chief of the eastern nome'. According to another interpretation the flail was originally a fly-whisk. The flail was always an attribute of the gods Osiris and Min. In the Old Kingdom it is already found on the backs of sacred animals. Kings also used the flail as a symbol of authority.

Flowers Flowers were presented to gods and deceased persons. When tied in a bouquet they served as offerings. The king was received with flowers in his triumphal homecoming. Sometimes the flowers were placed in holders in the shape of the ankh. This custom displays a deeper meaning. The gods were thought to be present in their bouquets, for divine fragrance was manifest in the scent of flowers. Flowers also carried gods on their petals – hence the fact that the creator god Harsomtus, in the form of a child or serpent, appeared on the lotus whilst Wadjet was called 'she who is upon her papyrus plant'. Hathor was also given this name in allusion to Wadjet. Lastly, one must mention the flower which stands upon a small temple behind the god Min.

In the Egyptian language the word for bouquet has the same consonantal framework as the word for life. Bouquets of flowers were a symbol of life and therefore played an important role in the cult of the dead. Scenes from the New Kingdom sometimes show a bouquet in place of the transfigured deceased, probably intended to show that the dead person had entered eternal spring. The flower was linked with the beginning of the world as a symbol of the unfolding of life, for the lotus was the flower which arose from the primeval waters. *See also* WREATH.

Fly In the Old and Middle Kingdoms the image of the fly had an amuletic character. This insect is found on magic wands. In the New Kingdom one sorcerer threatens, 'I will enter your body as a fly and see your body from the inside'. In accounts from the New Kingdom the fly appeared as a symbol of bravery because it was not easy to fend off, and soldiers who had proved themselves were decorated with the golden fly. Three large gold flies on a gold chain were found in the coffin of Queen Aahotep of the Seventeenth Dynasty, now in Cairo.

Four There were four cardinal points, hence the Pyramid Texts (No. 470) already mentioned a cosmic bull with four horns who guarded the roads of heaven. At the top of both sides of the Narmer palette are four faces with cow's horns; this was the sky-goddess who looked down from all sides onto the victory of her son, the king. The universality of the creator god Khnum was displayed in his fourfold nature for he was the *ba* of Re (heaven), of Shu (air), and Geb (Earth), and of Osiris (underworld), whilst as the *ba* of the same deities he was also described as the ram of Mendes. The number four furthermore had significance in the mortuary cult: four men pulled the coffin, all tools and vessels were in groups of four, likewise the canopic jars with the dead person's internal organs which were guarded by the four sons of Horus, whilst four goddesses, Isis, Nephthys, Neith and Selket, protected the canopic chest.

The sons of Horus were connected with the cardinal points: the human-headed Imsety with the south; ape-headed Hapi with the north; jackal-headed Duamutef with the east, and falcon-headed Qebsennuef with the west. The psychologist, C. G. Jung, pointed out the analogy with the vision of Ezekiel in which four cherubim, one in human form and three with animal faces among them a bird, represented the four cardinal points (Ezek. 1:10).

Fragrance Part of the nature of the gods was their 'pleasant scent'. The divine odour which was described as the 'fragrance of Punt' made the arrival of the divine manifest to the king. This delightful scent told the queen that Amun was approaching, in order to sleep with her.

As a divine characteristic, fragrance was itself imbued with the power of everlasting life, therefore the use of perfume and unguent played a part in cult over and above its cosmetic usage. One ancient text says, 'My scent is the scent of Horus, my odour is the odour of Horus'. In the antechamber of Tutankhamun's tomb several sealed jars were discovered. When they were opened in 1922 their delicate fragrance made it obvious that their intent was to give pleasant scents to the ruler in the next world along with the blessing which they emanated.

Frog The frog was a chthonic animal alluding to the forces which brought life into being. The male primeval gods of Hermopolis were often represented with frogs' heads. The frog was also the sacred animal of

Heket, the goddess of birth. The frog statuettes of faience, stone or ivory which were found in great numbers in the most ancient area of the temple of Khenti-Amentiu at Abydos could have been votive offerings to Heket. In the Middle Kingdom an image of a frog was applied to magical knives which were laid above the wombs of women or on new born children as a protection. The frog must also be mentioned in connection with later representations in which it was the companion of the Nile-god Hapi who assured fertility. In the Late Period the image of the frog became a symbol of rebirth, and was thus adopted by early Christians with the epithet, 'I am the Resurrection'.

G

Garden   The garden which Pharaoh, the Horus on earth, laid out was intended for his heavenly father. Queen Hatshepsut planted fragrant trees around the approaches to her mortuary temple at Deir el-Bahari, Thebes, intending it to be a garden for her father, the god Amun. Among the donations of Ramesses III to the temple of Heliopolis was a garden planted with trees and date palms, 'provided with lotuses, papyrus plants, reeds and flowers'. In a land surrounded by desert a garden giving fruit and shade was one of the most desirable earthly possessions, the enjoyment of which one wished to secure after death. The tomb inscription of the Vizier Rekhmire and his wife at Thebes runs thus: 'Take the lotus flowers which come from your garden. It has not been taken from you ... you refresh yourself in the shade of its trees and do what you like there unto all eternity'. In the tomb paintings of important officials of the Eighteenth and Nineteenth Dynasties scenes of gardens appear again and again. Sycamore, date and dom palms are most commonly depicted. The garden, an expressive image of life, became a symbol for survival after death. In the fields of the blest of the hereafter lay 'the divine city' (Book of the Dead, Chap. 110) where the 'eastern souls' dwelt together with the morning star.

Gazelle   In Komir in Upper Egypt, south of Esna, the gazelle was worshipped as the sacred animal of the goddess Anuket (Anukis

Gold head-dress of a minor wife of Tuthmosis III (1504–1450 BC) with the heads of two **Gazelles**, insignia of her standing, on the front of the circlet. They are mounted on two spigots, and removable. From Thebes. XVIII Dynasty. Metropolitan Museum of Art, New York, Purchase with Funds from Various Donors, 1926.

Relief of the earth god **Geb** shown swathed in a tight-fitting cloak. From a shrine to the pharaoh Zoser at Heliopolis. III Dynasty, *c.* 2670 BC. Museo Egizio, Turin.

in Greek). The goddess was almost always shown in human form. On one ostracon she was drawn in the form of a gazelle as 'lady of heaven' and 'mistress of the gods'. A ceremonial mace of King Narmer in the Ashmolean Museum, Oxford, depicts three gazelles in a paddock near a shrine which shows that the animal was worshipped in early times. It is uncertain what symbolic meaning was attached to the gazelle as a separate species since it belongs to the antelope genus. It was most probably an image of speed (the ancient Mesopotamian god Dumuzi transformed himself into a gazelle when he was fleeing), and in the case of Anuket it probably represented nimble grace. The gazelle occurs as insignia on the front of head-dresses of minor queens, or concubines, as the actual pieces from the Tomb of the Three Princesses of Tuthmosis III in the Metropolitan Museum, New York, and in the wall-painting of his daughters in the tomb of Menna at Thebes. The god Reshef, who was indigenous to Egypt after the Eighteenth Dynasty, wears a gazelle's head on his crown instead of a uraeus. As a hunted animal the gazelle was equated with Seth.

Geb Geb was the personification of the earth. In one Pyramid Text (No. 308) it states that the deceased entered into Geb. As god of the earth he bore the plants which grew on his back; water, too, sprang forth from him. According to an ancient myth Geb, together with the sky goddess Nut, produced the sun, hence he became the 'father of the gods'. He passed his earthly authority on to Osiris and then to Horus and finally to the king, who was therefore called 'heir of Geb'. Like all cosmic deities Geb was represented anthropomorphically; his sign, however, was a goose, for which reason Isis was once called 'egg of the goose'. Geb sometimes wore a goose on his head, but otherwise his headdress was the Lower Egyptian crown.

Gestures When hailing a deity a person knelt and inclined himself to the ground which he touched with his nose and forehead. This attitude was called 'kissing the ground'. When actually praying one knelt or more usually stood with arms raised and open palms extended towards the god. It cannot be proved whether the attitude of prayer, which involved the arms being outstretched sideways and bent up at right angles, bore a conscious connection to the *ka* sign. On seated statues of the Old Kingdom the stylized position of the hands was of special significance. In these the hand apparently placed on the knee reaches out to the food on the offering table (an attitude which is not seen in standing statues). This was evidently to attract renewed physical strength. The clenched fist of the other hand holds an amuletic band, the so-called blood of Isis, which hangs down. This characteristic attitude of the deceased during resurrection was adopted by later periods. In tomb paintings of the New Kingdom the left hand, now visible above rather than on the thigh, is extended towards the food whilst the right hand grasps either the shoulder band or a lotus flower, alluding to rebirth.

Goat The goat attained no great religious significance as the common man's sacrificial animal. Only in the town of Mendes, the Egyptian Djedet, was there an important goat cult. The sacred goat Ba-neb-Djedet, i.e. 'the billy-goat, lord of Djedet' was usually represented as a ram. The goat was a symbol of fertility, especially of generation, to whom women prayed in order to have children. Sacred goats were embalmed after death.

Gold Gold was regarded as a divine metal, especially in respect of the shining sun-god. The tops of obelisks were covered in sheet gold. The sky-goddess Hathor bore the epithet 'the golden one', or simply 'the gold', and it was said of the king, the son of the sun-god Re, that he was, 'the mountain of gold who irradiates the whole world'. Part of the royal titular contained the term 'golden Horus'. The immutability of the precious metal was a symbol of survival after death, although this was not especially emphasized. The royal tomb chambers and the workshops for coffins were called the 'House of Gold'. The mummy masks of the kings and many nomarchs were of pure gold. On the face masks of other people yellow symbolically took the place of gold. In the Late Period a 'vulture of gold which was placed round the neck of the transfigured one' was supposed to impart the protection of Isis. On the head and feet of New Kingdom sarcophagi the goddesses Isis and Nephthys were often represented kneeling on the sign for gold, which is seen in the picture as a necklace.

Goose Because of the symbolism of the egg the goose belonged to the area of creation myths, especially since egg-laying hens were not known until the time of Tuthmosis III's campaigns in Syria. The first god was supposed to have emerged from the egg of the 'great cackler'. This cosmic entity of primeval times was often equated with the primeval god, Amun; in fact, the god himself was sometimes depicted as a goose. In Graeco-Roman times the goose was found as an attribute of Harpocrates, i.e. Horus, the child. Since one often regarded the presentation of an offering as the annihilation of the enemies of the gods, and since the goose was one of the most popular sacrificial animals, it became the embodiment of evil powers and was regarded as an animal symbolic of Seth.

Grave goods All the various grave goods can be explained in the light of the concept that a life after death similar to that on earth could be possible, hence the discovery of food, tools and weapons in prehistoric and archaic tombs in Upper Egypt. Soon substitutes in the form of models of houses and ships, etc., sufficed, or even pictures which were to become magically effective for the deceased in the next world. From the end of the Old Kingdom the most important items of mortuary equipment were painted on the walls of sarcophagi and tomb chambers. Often these included items of regalia, which were to impart regal powers to the deceased on the other side. Friezes of objects, tools, cosmetic items, drinking vessels and food appear in the great wooden coffins of the Middle Kingdom.

Green 'To do green things' meant to generate goodness in contrast to doing 'red things' which meant to do evil. Green was regarded as the colour of vegetation, and of sprouting life. As a god of vegetation and resurrection, Osiris already bore the epithet 'the great green' in the Pyramid Texts (No. 628); this epithet was also used of the sea, which the Egyptians never felt quite sure of. Green malachite meant joy. Earlier mortuary literature describes the place of the blest as an eternal, freshly verdant 'field of malachite'. It is certainly not chance that the nurse of the child Horus, Wadjet, the green snake, was regarded as the 'papyrus-coloured one', for she guaranteed prosperity and protection to the divine child in the face of Seth's persecution. Since Wadjet was regarded as a manifestation of the Lower Egyptian crown, the latter was also termed 'green', although it really consisted of red cloth.

Griffon The leonine manifestation of the king, together with the falcon form of the sky-god Horus, were united in the image of the griffon. In the Old Kingdom the griffon was already a symbol of the victorious ruler who strode across the twitching bodies of his enemies. In Ptolemaic and Roman times the sun-gods, Horus and Re, were represented as griffons. As a demonic entity with a winged lion's body and falcon's head the griffon already appeared on magic wands of the New Kingdom; reined to a chariot he led the hunter to victory over typhonic animals. In the Late Period the griffon was regarded as the 'mightiest of animals' and as a symbol of retributive justice, until the Ptolemies eventually identified him with Nemesis.

Ground plan One may distinguish two types of architecture erected for the gods or the deceased.

1 The axial type, especially prevalent in temple plans. The axis leads through the two pylons in the forecourt, which was flooded with light, and from there to the bright inner courtyard, thence into the gloomy hypostyle hall beyond which stood the portal of the sanctuary, wreathed in darkness. In there loomed the divine image, to which only the high priests had access. The gloom increased to reach a climax of utter darkness, in the same way that the mood of the man who enjoyed the light darkened when he turned from the world to expose himself to the profound depths of the divine.

2 The labyrinth or spiral plan. Temples and tombs were images of mythical places and reproduced their winding paths. It is in this light that one must see the twisting corridors which were hewn in the earlier tombs of the New Kingdom in the Valley of the Kings, and also the passage skirting the sanctuary in temples. *See also* PYRAMID; TEMPLE

H

Relief carved in the tomb of Seti I (1318–1304 BC) showing him wearing the costume of the High Priest of Ptah of Memphis. His **Hair** is dressed in an ornamental side-lock, part of the insignia of his office. His prenomen, Men-Maat-Ra, is cut in the cartouche before him. XIX Dynasty. Tomb no. 17 in the Valley of the Kings, Thebes.

Hair Hair is regarded by many nations as a receptacle for physical and often secret power (cf. the Biblical tale of Samson). Whenever the Egyptian king conquered an enemy the fact was made plain by his seizing him by a tuft of hair. Grabbing hold of the hair symbolized the subjection of the whole person. When Isis cut off a lock of hair in mourning for Osiris that, too, was a symbolic gesture; also the determinative for the word 'mourning' consisted of three locks of hair. It is questionable as to how far one should connect this with the shaven heads of priests, which symbolized subjection to divine power; texts from earlier times already called them 'bald-headed ones'. To shave the head as an hygienic requirement is referred to by Herodotus.

According to ancient tradition boys wore a long, plaited side-lock on the right side of the head; the hieroglyph for this object, in fact, meant 'child'. In pictorial representations the lock of hair was a special mark of the child Horus, of the royal princes, and also of the High Priest of Ptah of Memphis. A reference in the Book of the Dead (Chap. 115) to the side-lock may have alluded to eternal youth, since the deceased says 'I know why a tress is made for a male'.

Hand To ancient peoples the hand was symbol of creative power. Egyptian representations show Ptah, the 'fashioner of the earth' forming the egg of the world with his hands on a potter's wheel in the same way as Khnum models the body of the child. According to the Heliopolitan cosmogony the first creatures, Shu and Tefnut, came into being from the semen which the primeval god produced with his hand. In this case the hand signified the female element inherent in god-head which was made into an independent entity in historical times. In the Herakleopolitan period coffins displayed the divine couple 'Atum and his hand'. Eventually the 'god's hand' became a title for the fictitious wife of Amun, i.e. for the queen or a princess, who it was hoped would bear an heir to the throne. A well-known motif in Amarna art was the sun-disc, the Aten, whose rays were extended in blessing and terminated in hands. After the Old Kingdom the hand served as an amulet for averting demons.

Hapi The god of the Nile in inundation, who was especially worshipped at Elephantine and Gebel Silsileh, both areas of turbulent water by virtue of the First Cataract and whirlpools in the river, respectively. He was thought to dwell in a cavern from which the Nile flowed forth − the annual inundation was called the 'arrival of Hapi'. Representations show Hapi as a long-haired naked man with heavy pendulous breasts and with a clump of papyrus on his head; he carries laden offering tables.

Hare The hare was the sacred animal of Wenet who was worshipped in the fifteenth Upper Egyptian nome. This anthropomorphic goddess wore a standard on her head with a recumbent hare. Figures of hares of the Late Period had amuletic significance. According to Plutarch the Egyptians

Relief of the Nile god Hapi shown kneeling holding an offering table loaded with fruit and ducks. In his left hand he holds the long stems of papyrus plants, the symbol of Lower Egypt, and below the offering table hang lotus flowers, the symbol of Upper Egypt. XIX Dynasty, c. 1310 BC. Temple of Seti I, Abydos.

The façade of the great Ptolemaic temple dedicated to the cow goddess **Hathor** at Dendera. The head of the goddess is carved at the top of the pillars above the screens and also on those of the hypostyle hall inside. The temple was begun under Ptolemy IX (116–107 BC) and added to by later Ptolemies and Roman emperors up until Trajan (AD 98–117).

esteemed the hare as a symbol of divine qualities because of its swiftness and its acute senses. The relationship of the hare to Osiris, which has been variously affirmed, is unexplained. If a proof could be found then this would presumably have something to do with the moon, since in many nations the hare was a lunar animal, for example, among the Chinese and Aztecs.

Haroeris   *see* HORUS

Harpocrates   *see* HORUS

Hathor   The name of this goddess means 'house of Horus'; her sign corresponds to this since it depicts a falcon in a house. In earlier times the sky goddess was regarded as the mother of the sun-god until Isis replaced her. The concept of the sky as a cow, which was widespread in the Delta, causes Hathor to be given bovine form. An Eighteenth Dynasty sculpture from Deir el-Bahari, now in the Egyptian Museum, in Cairo, shows Hathor as a cow protecting the king. Usually the goddess was shown in human form wearing on her head the sun-disc flanked by a cow's horns. According to an ancient myth Hathor was supposed to have raised the youthful sun up to heaven by means of her horns. In the end the goddess who bore the sun was herself equated with the sun, being regarded as the solar eye.

In the Old Kingdom Dendera was already Hathor's main cult centre; this was heavily reinforced later when the great Ptolemaic temple dedicated to her was built there. Her cult symbol was a round pillar surmounted by two cow's heads or two female heads. The goddess was regarded as the 'female soul with two faces'. In Thebes Hathor in bovine form was worshipped as a mortuary goddess. The dying person wished to be 'in the following of Hathor' who also received the setting sun and, like herself, preserved it from the powers of darkness. One of her most common attributes was the sistrum, a rattle-like instrument. Hathor was also goddess of dance, music and love.

Hat-mehit A minor fish goddess of Mendes in the Delta, a town better known for its ram-headed god. She is usually represented as a woman with a fish on her head.

Head When the deceased prays in the Book of the Dead (Chap. 53) that 'I will not walk upside down', this is an image of death. Below some scenes in the third corridor of the tomb of Ramesses IX is a frieze depicting men standing on their heads. In the Book of the Netherworld, Amduat, it is related how fire-spitting demons annihilate, at the sun god's behest, the 'shadows', 'heads' and 'those who are placed on their heads'. The fear of damage being done to the mummy and thereby losing one's head led in the Old Kingdom to the practice of placing a life-sized reserve head in the tomb. The mummy mask which appeared in the New Kingdom was likewise a means of assurance against the possible loss of one's head.

Head-cloth The head-cloth of the king was a symbol of the Upper Egyptian national goddess Nekhbet, a fact which is referred to in the Pyramid Texts (No. 729). When the king went into battle he was accompanied and protected by the vulture 'with the white head-dress'. *See also* CROWNS.

Head-dresses The head-dress was an important attribute of Egyptian gods, but was not always enough to identify them, since when the nature of one god coloured another their emblems interchanged. The most important head-dresses were:

Amentet (personification of the west) – an abbreviated standard with a feather and bird on top (the hieroglyphic sign for 'west').
Amun – crown of two plumes.
Anhur – crown of four plumes.
Anuket (mistress of the Nile) – feathered crown.
Atum – the double crown.
Geb – a combination of the Lower Egyptian crown and the Atef crown. Also a goose.
Ha (god of the western desert) – 'hilly' country (the hieroglyphic sign for 'desert').
Hathor – cow's horns and solar disc.
Heh (personification for everlastingness and eternity) – a palm frond.
Hemsut (a protective goddess) – the shield with two arrows crossed over it.
Horus – the double crown or double crown of feathers.
Iabet (personification of the east) – a spear decked out as a standard, (the hieroglyphic sign for 'east').
Isis – cow's horns and solar disc, or vulture head-dress, or the hieroglyphic sign for 'throne'.
Khons – the moon disc and crescent.
Maat – ostrich feather.
Meshkent (goddess of birth) – a blade of grass or corn split and rolled over at the end.
Min – crown of double plumes with streamer hanging down the back.
Mut – vulture head-dress, often surmounted by the double crown.
Nefertem – lotus flower.
Nekhbet – vulture head-dress or Upper Egyptian crown.
Neith – shield with two arrows, which could also be a quiver, and the Lower Egyptian crown.
Nephthys – a rectangular enclosure seen in plan, surmounted by a wickerwork basket (the hieroglyphic sign for 'Lady of the house').
Nut – rounded pot.
Osiris – Atef crown.
Ptah – Mummy's skull cap.
Reshef – the Upper Egyptian Crown with a gazelle's head instead of a uraeus.
Satis – crown with two antelope horns.
Selket – scorpion.
Seshat – a seven or five-pointed star.
Shu – ostrich feather.

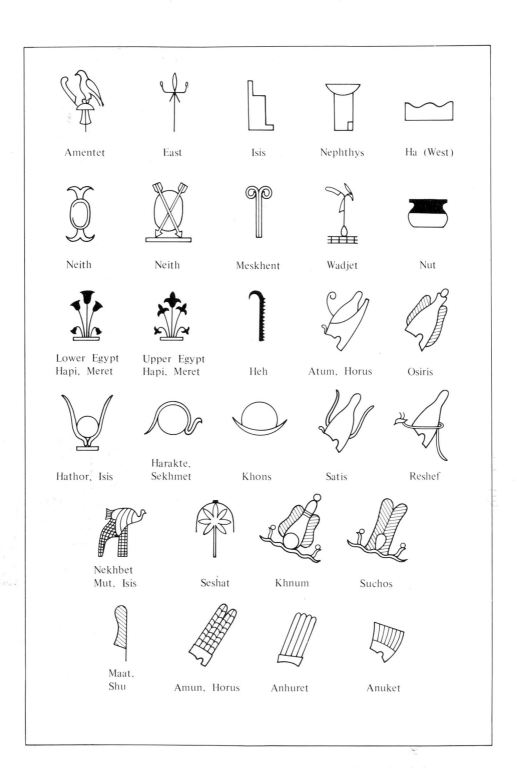

Amentet   East   Isis   Nephthys   Ha (West)

Neith   Neith   Meskhent   Wadjet   Nut

Lower Egypt Hapi, Meret   Upper Egypt Hapi, Meret   Heh   Atum, Horus   Osiris

Hathor, Isis   Harakte, Sekhmet   Khons   Satis   Reshef

Nekhbet Mut, Isis   Seshat   Khnum   Suchos

Maat, Shu   Amun, Horus   Anhuret   Anuket

When not identified by the inscription accompanying them most Egyptian gods and goddesses can be identified by their individual **Head-dresses**, although at times several deities can share the same type.

Waset (the goddess of the Theban nome) – a *was*-sceptre decorated with a ribbon and feather surmounting the sign for 'nome' (a criss-crossed grid signifying land marked out with irrigation runnels).

Heart The heart was a symbol of life. When the heart wearied the body died. Osiris whose 'heart is listless' lay in the sleep of death and it was said of the deceased that his heart had 'departed', for without that central organ life after death was unthinkable. The heart was left in its place during embalming, although all other inner organs were removed. Spells from the Book of the Dead were supposed to guarantee that the deceased would receive his heart back in the other world: 'See, this heart of mine, it weeps in the presence of Osiris and pleads for mercy!' (Chap. 28). In the Hall of Judgement before Osiris and the 42 judges of the dead the heart of the deceased is placed on the scales. A person's true character was revealed in his heart which was entreated not to rise up against the deceased so that, as he said, 'my name may not stink and appear rotten to the ruler in the next world'. The scene of the 'Weighing of the Heart' was a popular representation in Books of the Dead. The heart scarab which was laid on the mummy wrapped within the bandages was an amulet designed to prevent the heart from making an unfavourable utterance. It was usually inscribed with Chapter 30 of the Book of the Dead. The heart was also the seat of the emotions and intellect. The primeval god, Ptah, conceived the universe in his heart and gave it substance by means of his creative word.

Heaven *see* LADDER OF HEAVEN; SUPPORTERS OF HEAVEN

Hedjet *see* CROWNS

Heh In numbers Heh denotes a million, and so he came to be used in expressing a good wish for 'millions of years' of life, stability, etc. He is normally shown kneeling and holding a notched palm rib in his hands.

Heker The so-called heker was a representation of the knots with which plant stems were fastened to a wooden frame to serve as a wall. These signs were placed on the walls of temples and tomb chambers near the ceiling and were not only for decoration but also had symbolic significance, for they alluded to the primeval home of the god, the national

Underside of a large felspar **Heart** scarab inscribed with the 30th Chapter of the Book of the Dead, whereby the heart of the deceased shall not be taken from him. New Kingdom. Ashmolean Museum, Oxford.

Engraved back of a gold pectoral of the princess Sit-Hathor-Iunet. The god **Heh** kneels holding notched palm-ribs, signifying a count of years, and has a frog, symbol of 100,000, hanging from his left arm. The falcons on either side of him link via uraei looped through ankh signs with the prenomen of the king, Kheper-ka-Ra (Senusret II, 1897–1878 BC). From Lahun. XII Dynasty. Metropolitan Museum of Art, New York, Rogers Fund and contribution of Henry Walters, 1916.

Part of the 'Campbell' papyrus, the Book of the Dead of Pinedjem II and his wife Neskhons. The left-hand side is written in the **Hieratic** script whilst on the right the text above Pinedjem is in normal hieroglyphic script. Pinedjem is shown offering a flame to a standing, swathed figure of Osiris who wears the atef crown and has a menat hanging down his back. He holds a crook and flail and a long sceptre that combines the *was* and djed-pillar at its head. From Deir el-Bahari. XXI Dynasty, *c.* 1000 BC. British Museum.

shrine. The heker therefore harks back to the 'first time' in which the gods ruled Egypt.

Heket The goddess Heket, who was represented in the form of a frog or with a frog's head, was worshipped especially in the town of Her-wer as the female complement of Khnum. Together with other gods she assisted in fashioning the child in the womb and presided over the birth in her capacity of midwife. On account of her life-giving powers she was classified at Abydos among the Osirian family of deities. Depictions of later times show her present at the posthumous conception of Horus.

Herdsman The images of herdsman and shepherd are implicit in the instruction of Merikare (Tenth Dynasty) when he calls mankind 'the small cattle of god' who are well cared for by the beneficence of their lord. There exists a eulogy of Amun from the Ramesside Period in which the god looks after his cattle like a conscientious herdsman. Re 'acts as shepherd in his herbage', and men and animals breathed the air and drank of the water which he gave them. It is obvious that the king who led his people was viewed as a shepherd, rather as in Mesopotamia. Pharaoh's insignia originated, via Osiris, from the ancient royal god Anedjti who, at the same time, had the characteristics of a divine shepherd. The crook was originally a shepherd's crook. It is disputed as to whether the so-called 'flail' was a shepherd's whip.

Hieratic The hieratic script was a cursive development of the hieroglyphic script, a simplification of the original signs to aid speed in writing. It was suited and especially used for writing on papyrus and much of the surviving legal, literary and religious documents are in this script. It first appears early in the Old Kingdom and is regularly used until shortly after the end of the New Kingdom (*c.* 800 BC). Although initially often written in vertical columns, it later tended to be written horizontally from right to left. It developed its own style as it moved further away from the original hieroglyphic signs, making it more difficult to read. A late form known as 'abnormal hieratic' is far distant from its origins, and extremely difficult to understand. *See also* DEMOTIC; HIEROGLYPHS.

Hieroglyphs The Egyptian language only possessed a single word for 'writing' and 'drawing', which proves the close connection between script and image. In an Old Kingdom text the hieroglyphs were given the general term 'gods', for in them the intangible was supposed to become graphic. Several ancient ideograms retained their original symbolic value, for example, the sign for heaven (a roof); god (perhaps a flag on a pole, or an axe); sun and horizon, (a mountain with a sun); life, soul (a bird); power (a lion-headed gaming piece); strength, happiness, gold (a necklace), also the words for ruler, festival and gifts.

The hieroglyphic signs for the gods are true symbols: the falcon for Horus, the throne for Isis, a desert animal with an arrow-like tail for Seth, a shield with crossed arrows for Neith, a combination of the signs for house and lady for Nephthys, and a jackal on a naos for Anubis. Signs formed by analogy were also symbolic to a certain extent, thus the colour red, and blood also, were represented with the picture of a flamingo, and green, which meant prosperity was denoted by the papyrus plant. Egyptian writing was divided into three types of signs:

1. Ideograms rendered a certain word without reference to its sound. A rectangle with an opening below meant 'house', a billowing sail 'wind', whilst two legs signified 'to walk'. The lotus or reed, characteristic of Upper Egypt, meant 'south'. The conjoined signs for 'god' and 'servant' meant 'priest', whilst the goose, the phonogram for 'son', together with the sun stood for the king, as 'son of the sun'. The ankh signified 'life' which, together with the sign for 'lord', denoted the coffin and were a symbolic expression of the hope of overcoming death.

2. Phonograms reproduced one consonant or a succession of two or three consonants whilst the vowels remained unwritten. Therefore the image of the goose (s3) was also used to write 'son' since this word had the same consonantal framework. A swallow (wr) served to write the word 'great' (wr), and a beetle (ḫpr) was used for 'to become' (ḫpr). The ideogram of the vulture was employed as the phonogram for 'mother; the basket for 'Lord'; the club (ḥm) for servant, and the flywhisk (ms) for 'to give birth' (msi). Words of one consonant could also be used as single letters thus the stool (p) stood for 'p', the loaf (t) for 't', the mouth (r) for 'r', the water (nw) for 'n', the lake (š) for 'sh' and the hand (drt) for 'd'.

3. Determinatives had no phonetic value. They were placed at the end of a word to indicate its category. Thus the names of towns included the ideogram for town. The locust was determined with the sign for bird

Scenes of hunting the **Hippopotamus** in the marshes are a favourite representation in the mastaba tombs of the nobles of the Old Kingdom. In this scene, from the mastaba of Ti at Sakkara, boatmen are busy spearing the beasts whilst one of the hippopotami has grasped a crocodile in its powerful jaws, intent on breaking its back. Both animals signified evil elements to the ancient Egyptian. V Dynasty, c. 2380 BC.

(goose) because both fly. Abstract words, for example, qualities, contained an added papyrus scroll; mammals, the image of a skin with attached tail, whilst three strokes of the same length indicated the plural. *See also* DEMOTIC; HIERATIC.

Hippopotamus There was already a festival of this animal in the Old Kingdom in Lower Egypt at which the king slaughtered a white hippopotamus. As a result of this the king was soon regarded as Horus, killing Seth who was in animal form. It is certainly in the light of this that one must see the wall paintings of the New Kingdom and, for example, the small gold-covered statuettes of the king spearing from the tomb of Tutankhamun. In the temple of Edfu several reliefs show Horus stabbing 'the wretched one in hippopotamine shape' with a spear. Because all true symbols are ambivalent, the hippopotamus can appear in a good light. The wooden frames of New Kingdom funerary beds were shaped like hippopotami; here this thick-skinned creature had apotropaic significance. Apart from this the hippopotamus was regarded as a symbol of female fertility and manifested herself in the form of the protective goddess Taweret. Mention must also be made of the fine hippopotamus figurines of blue faience from Middle Kingdom tombs.
See illustration on p. 63.

Hoeing the ground Hoeing the ground was for the Egyptian a symbolic act of offering. At the feast of the mortuary god, Sokar, who was affected by Osirian concepts, black oxen pulled the plough whilst a boy planted barley, flax and spelt. Myth relates how Seth and his confederates in the form of goats wanted to interfere with the task of hoeing the divine field at Busiris, but the gods who guarded Osiris killed the goats and fertilized the earth with their blood. The rite of hoeing the ground alluded to the death of Osiris who was put into the earth in the symbolic form of corn. When at Busiris goats were finally driven across the field at sowing time in order to trample in the corn, it was a conscious reference to typhonic forces. The rite of hoeing the ground was a symbolic expression of the death and burial of Osiris and the germinating corn alluded to resurrection.

Horizon The sign for the Egyptian word (*3ḫt*) was a mountain with two peaks, between which the sun emerged. The horizon was also the place of sunrise or sunset. Akhet

On a limestone mace-head king Scorpion (with his sign before his face) is shown wearing the White Crown of Upper Egypt and symbolically **Hoeing** earth into a basket held before him by a retainer. From Hierakonpolis. I Dynasty, *c.* 3100 BC. Ashmolean Museum, Oxford.

was the home of the sun-god who, as the rising sun, normally bore the name Herakhty, Horus of the Horizon. The new city which Akhenaten built was called Akhetaten (The Horizon of Aten), the present day Tell el Amarna. In the end the horizon became a metaphor for the temple and the royal palace, the former being described as the 'horizon in which Re dwells'.

Horn The ram's head was regarded in the hieroglyphic script as an expression of respectful fear and might. In conjunction with the crown, horns were used as the head-dress of many deities, whilst ordinary people regarded it as the embodiment of the fear surrounding the supernatural. The ram-headed god, Khnum, was usually represented with horizontally projecting horns whilst those of the ram of Amun were curved downward, although there are numerous representations with lateral horns. Mauritanian and Algerian rock drawings show rams or buffalo with the sun-disc between their horns. There are also representations of the anthropomorphic Amun wearing the sun-disc or uraeus, symbol of the sun, on his head.

Bulls and cows were particularly regarded as representatives of the sun, the bull because it could symbolize the sun itself and the cow because, as a symbol of the night and the moon, she caused the solar disc to emerge from her body; in this connection one must allude to the device widespread in Western Asia of the cow's horns and the crescent moon which corresponded to the microcosm and macrocosm. According to Plutarch, Isis, a lunar goddess, was the mother of the sun-god Horus. Her head was often surmounted by a cow's horn and sun-disc, a mode of representation which actually belonged to Hathor. One myth tells how Hathor raised the young sun-god to heaven on her horns.

Horus In the beginning Horus was imagined to be a sky god whose image was seen as that of a falcon with outstretched wings, whose eyes were regarded as the sun and moon. Already at the beginning of the early historic period the celestial falcon was equated with the king. To his people the ruler was a manifestation of Horus. The Horus name of the king was written inside a *serekh* ('palace façade'), surmounted by a falcon. Since not only the sky, but the sun also, were seen as a falcon, the king, sun and sky became identified and this found its final expression as the royal symbol of the winged disc.

Seti I greets the falcon-headed **Horus** who wears the sun-disc encircled by the royal uraeus on his head. Here he is shown in a particular aspect as Re-Herakhty, Horus of the Horizon. XIX Dynasty, *c.* 1310 BC. Tomb of Seti I, no. 17 in the Valley of the Kings, Thebes.

Green-glazed faience plaque representing the pharaoh Yewepet as the child-king **Horus**, holding a flail, finger to mouth and wearing an ornate triple atef crown. He squats on a lotus flower, symbolic of the marshes in which Isis reared the young Horus. From Thebes. XXIII Dynasty, *c.* 725 BC. Royal Scottish Museum, Edinburgh.

Because of the Egyptians' dualistic world view Horus gained a rival in his uncle, Seth. Horus lost an eye in the battle between them, but in the end the two deities were reconciled in rulership over the 'land of the Nile'. Seth usually appeared as a god of Upper Egypt and Horus as a god of Lower Egypt. In later times Horus was regarded as ruler of all Egypt, whilst Seth merely remained god of the infertile desert and of barbaric peoples. When the cult of Osiris assumed precedence Horus became the son of Osiris and the nephew of Seth. As Harsiese (Greek version of the Egyptian 'Horus, son of Isis') he grew up in the seclusion of the Delta marshes, later to avenge his father, Osiris, as Harendotes.

Another form of Horus was Harpocrates, i.e. 'Horus the child', who had a young boy's head with the side-lock of youth and his finger in his mouth. In Graeco-Roman times he was numbered among the most popular divinities of the common people and was represented in various specialized forms in bronze and clay, for example, as a sun child on a lotus blossom or with a pot as bringer of fertility. Small plaques, known as cippi of Horus, show him standing on a crocodile and often associated with many and various other symbols of deities. These were very popular in houses to ward off evil spirits and the evil eye. Horus' important cult centres were at Edfu, where the god was venerated in the image of the winged disc; Kom Ombo, where as son of Re he bore the name Haroeris, and Heliopolis, where he was regarded as the god of the morning sun under the name of Re-Herakhty.

Children of Horus   In the Pyramid Texts the four children of Horus appear as pathfinders at the ascension of the dead. Because there were four of them they were linked with the four cardinal points, and it was with this in mind that their picture, or simply their names, were retained on the four corners of coffins in the Middle Kingdom. Their task was to protect the body above all from hunger and thirst, especially the inner organs which were most affected. *See also* CANOPIC JARS.

In the vignette to Chapter 125 of the Book of the Dead (the 'negative Confession'), the four sons of Horus were shown in human form standing on a lotus flower. Their origin in the primeval cosmic flower was a symbolic allusion to the rebirth of the deceased from the lotus which their power would effect.

Eye of Horus The sun and moon were mythically imagined to be the eyes of the god Horus. The term 'eye of Horus' (singular) is understood to refer to the moon although the distinction between it and the eye of Re, i.e. the sun, is no less equivocal. The eye of Horus fought the enemies of the light and was itself seen as fire. In the Book of the Dead (Chap. 42) the text states that, 'I am one who is with the Sound Eye; even when closed I am in its protection'. The myth tells how the eye of the moon was lost in a battle against Seth and then recovered. It was this eye which Horus presented to his father Osiris, thereby helping him to attain new life; the presentation of the eye of Horus was regarded in Egypt as the archetype of every offering ceremony. After the New Kingdom the lotus god, Nefertum, was often depicted with the eye of Horus in one hand, a symbolic allusion to the oblation which usually consisted of food and drink, from where Nefertum derived the name 'lord of sustenance'.

Spear of Horus The mythical weapon of the royal deity, Horus, was a spear which had been blessed by the goddess Neith. In an ancient text it is said of the spear, 'Its barbs are the rays of the sun, its tips are the claws of Mafdet', i.e. the goddess of punishment. Horus, also called the 'harpooner', hunted typhonic powers in the shape of hippopotami with his divine weapon and is thus represented on the walls of his great temple at Edfu. Small models of the spear were often placed with the dead in the tomb as a protection on the road to the next world.

House Along with vessels, the house was part of the maternal symbolism of hollow spaces. In the Egyptian language the house was at the same time an image for the womb. Hathor was called 'house of Horus', Nut 'the house of devouring', and Nekhbet was regarded as the 'lady of the great house', which was the national shrine of Upper Egypt at El Kab. The name Nephthys meant 'lady of the house' or 'lady of the estate'. Protection and preservation were part of the elementary female characteristics; vessel, house and tomb therefore alluded to the central themes of female life; birth, marriage and death. Isis lamented for the dead Osiris and wished to call him back with the words, 'Come to your house, come to your house, O pillar! Come to your house, beautiful bull, Lord of mankind, beloved lord of women!' According to more recent psychological interpretation the pillar of Osiris is to be seen

Small bronze cippus of **Horus** showing him as a naked youth, with the side-lock of hair of youth, standing on the backs of two crocodiles. Above his head is a grotesque face of the dwarf-god Bes, and in his hand he holds two long sceptres, one topped by plumes the other by a Horus-falcon wearing the Double Crown. Late Ptolemaic or Roman period. Musée d'Art et d'Histoire, Geneva.

as Osiris' lost phallus. Such a view would also explain the nature of the god Iuwenmutef, 'pillar of his mother'. This would be a synonym for Kamutef, 'bull of his mother', itself an epithet of Min, a concept which defined the fertility god as his own begetter.

Human sacrifice One representation which originates from the Archaic Period was that of the king triumphing over his enemies whom he seizes by the hair while delivering a fatal blow with his mace. These representations, which later were particularly common on temple pylons, only had a symbolic character. Human sacrifice, however, was certainly practised in the Predynastic Period. Discoveries in several cemeteries have proved that it was still customary in the First Dynasty to kill servants and slave women at the king's funeral, so that they would stand ready to help their lord in the next world. Later, in the Middle Kingdom, wooden models acted as substitute figures, followed in the New Kingdom by ushabtis. Substitute human sacrifice is known to have been practised in the Pyramid Age for clay figures of bound men and pottery bowls inscribed with the names of hostile chieftains were smashed to pieces. One seal seems to point to a changeover from the original sacrifice of human beings to that of animals; affixed to the chosen animal, it showed a kneeling man with hands tied behind his back and a knife at his throat.

An example of a well-wrapped mummy of the sacred **Ibis**, from the sacred animal necropolis at Sakkara. The appliqué on the outside of the wrappings represents the god Nefertem wearing a lotus crown. Many thousands of mummified ibises have been found in recent years in the underground galleries beneath Third Dynasty tombs. Ptolemaic period. British Museum.

I

Ibis The sacred ibis (*ibis religiosa*) was a white bird with black on its head, neck and the tips of the wing pinions. It attained special significance because it was regarded as the incarnation of Thoth. Numerous mummified ibises were laid to rest in the necropolis of Hermopolis, Thoth's main cult centre. Thousands of examples have also been found in the sacred animal necropolis at Sakkara. They were specially bred on the nearby lake at Abusir to be embalmed and offered to pilgrims to dedicate in the vast underground galleries of the site. The crested ibis (*ibis comata*), with dark iridescent plumage, is seen in the written character for the word 'to be radiant' and in earlier times it appeared as a metaphor for 'transfiguration', and, lastly, as an image for the transfigured dead.

Ichneumon The ichneumon (mongoose) appeared relatively late among sacred animals. Ichneumon gods in the mortuary temple of Amenemhet III and in Ramesside tombs signified spirits of the netherworld. In the Lower Egyptian town of Letopolis the ichneumon was equated with Horus. Ichneumon figures, used as votive offerings, bore the solar disc on their heads. It was related that Re, the sun-god, had once transformed himself into an ichneumon in order to fight Apophis, the serpent of the netherworld. Then the ichneumon was identified with the national goddess of Lower Egypt, Wadjet, and wore the sun-disc with a uraeus.

Bronze figure of an **Ibis**, the bird sacred to the god Thoth. Saite-Ptolemaic period. British Museum.

Image Aesthetic standpoints played no role in the artistic activity of the Egyptians. Painting and sculpture were only significant in respect of magic but not in themselves. The sculptor was called 'he who causes to live' and his work was described by the word 'to give birth'. Images were not merely lifelike copies, they were imbued with life, or preserved the existence of the person represented for an endless period. If a person's mummy should rot or be violated despite all the precautions, then the *ka*, the second self, could find refuge in an image of complete resemblance to himself. Statues could also be set up as votive offering in temples to enable the deceased to participate in the lifegiving rituals. Tomb paintings served to perpetuate the property of the deceased into eternity. What the westerner might call a symbol was reality to the Egyptian. Divine images were also real. Thus it was said of Amun, 'his soul is in heaven, his body in the West', i.e. the land of the dead, 'but his image is in his cult centre'. Of Osiris it was said, 'he comes as a spirit ... he sees his sanctuary. He sees his secret form painted in its place, his figure carved into the wall. Then he enters his secret form and alights upon his image'.

Bronze figure of an **Ichneumon** ('Pharaoh's rat'). From Thebes. XXVI Dynasty, 663–525 BC. British Museum.

Imhotep The vizier and chief architect of the pharaoh Zoser of the Third Dynasty who built the Step Pyramid, the first monumental stone building in the world, at Sakkara, *c.* 2670 BC. His fame was such that some two thousand years after his death he was deified, an unusual practice in ancient Egypt.

Bronze statuette of the deified **Imhotep**. He is normally represented seated like this with an open roll of papyrus on his lap. The scroll, and the base of the statuette, generally carry an inscription recording the name and titles of the donor of the statuette. Late Period. Egyptian Museum, Cairo.

Imhotep became a god of medicine and healing and was identified with Aesculapius by the Greeks. Representations of him, invariably small bronze votive figurines of the Late Period, show him seated with an open papyrus scroll across his lap. At the small Ptolemaic temple built at Deir el-Medineh by Ptolemy IV, Imhotep was worshipped along with Hathor and Maat and Amenhetep-son-of-Hapu, the latter also a deified architect. In the Late Period and into classical times there was a cult centre of Imhotep at Sakkara where pilgrims came to dedicate mummified animals, especially wrapped and decorated ibises, in the catacombs that extended under the mastaba tombs of the Third Dynasty nobles. Professor W. B. Emery spent many years up until his death in 1971 searching for the tomb of Imhotep among the great mastaba tombs of the Third Dynasty to the north-east of the Step Pyramid. The tombs had mostly been cleared and purified with clean sand in Ptolemaic times and their shafts gave access into the catacombs excavated beneath them. Generally, early tombs of this period are not decorated or inscribed and can only be allocated to an owner on the evidence of jar-sealings with names, etc., most of which had been removed in the later clearance. One particular mastaba (No. 3517) is larger than the rest (56 × 25 m.) and shares exactly the same orientation as the Step Pyramid; it is not possible, however, categorically to ascribe it to Imhotep. *See also* DEIFICATION.

Imiut The term 'imiut' referred in the beginning to an ancient fetish which already appears on First Dynasty monuments. It consisted of a headless animal skin hung on a pole which was stuck into a pot. In the very early period imiut was planted in the ground by the king's throne as a sign of protection. A personified imiut handed the king the sceptre of power at his heb-sed festival. In the Pyramid Texts the way was being paved for its assimilation with the god of cemeteries, Anubis, for both were called 'son of the Hesat-cow'. Wooden images of imiut were occasionally placed in the tombs of distinguished personages, and good examples were found in the tomb of Tutankhamun.

Imsety *see* CANOPIC JARS

Inversion An ancient conception of the kingdom of the dead was that it was upside down. It is known from the Coffin Texts and the Book of the Dead that the Egyptians feared being placed on their heads in the netherworld. In the Book of Caverns there are several scenes showing the god's enemies standing on their heads, some pleading for mercy, some as bound female figures, some as headless criminals, and some as *ba*-birds as independent manifestations of the deceased. All are in the primeval darkness and are unable to see the rays of the sun. For the dead the other side was a topsy-turvy world, hence the fact that the ferryman of the netherworld was called 'backface' because he looked in the wrong direction. In the judgement scene in the fifth hour of Amduat there are four inverted antelope heads above the enthroned Osiris, which are called 'roarer' as symbols of retributive power. In the twelfth hour of the Book of the Gates, and also on the sarcophagus of Seti I, the sky-goddess (the entrance to the netherworld), stands with her feet uppermost on the head of Osiris who encircles the land of the dead.

The hope of the dead for survival rested in the idea of inversion. His earthly life passed from childhood to old age, from birth to death. Therefore he hoped for rejuvenation, to move in reverse from death to life. In the Book of the Earth the sun was held up as an example of the miracle of rebirth, for it travelled in its barque in the opposite direction with the stern foremost from the realm of night into new morning.

Ished-tree The ished was one of the sacred trees. It was a fruit-bearing, deciduous species. The 'holy ished in the house of obelisks' at Heliopolis was famous. It was said of Re that he split the ished-tree one morning after defeating his enemies, a metaphor for the opening of the horizon and sunrise. In the temple at Dendera a relief on the ceiling shows two isheds on the tops of two mountains flanking the rising sun. The ished became significant as a tree of life on the leaves of which Thoth and the goddess Seshat wrote the regnal years of the king, thus placing him under divine protection during his reign. This was a popular motif in the Ramesside period.

Isis This goddess's name probably meant 'seat' or 'throne' and was written with a sign identical to the one which she wore on her head. Isis could therefore originally have been the embodiment of the throne. She was of special significance for the king, being regarded as his symbolic mother. In myth she sought her dead husband and brother, Osiris, conceived her son Horus by him,

The common statuettes of the goddess **Isis**, generally in bronze or faience, show her seated suckling the infant Horus. Here, on a side screen on a mammisi (birth house) built by the Roman emperor Augustus (27 BC–AD 14), she is shown standing, embracing and suckling the young god who wears the side-lock of youth. He is seen in another aspect behind her, sucking his finger. Before her the Roman emperor in the guise of an Egyptian pharaoh wearing the Red Crown makes an offering to the deities. Mammisi within the temenos wall of the temple at Dendera.

buried him and mourned him together with her sister Nephthys. The lamenting goddesses were also symbolically represented in the form of two birds of prey (kites). They are seen on the sides of coffins in human form and with outstretched wings, protecting the deceased and wafting the power of life towards him. In the second hour of Amduat the two goddesses were represented as two snakes rearing up in the bows of the solar barque facing in the direction of the journey.

Isis was worshipped as the 'great of magic' who had protected her son Horus from snakes, predators and other dangers; thus she would protect mortal children also. Orion was regarded as the soul of Osiris, hence astrologers imagined Sirius, whom the Egyptians called Sopdu and the Greeks Sothis, to be Isis. In the New Kingdom Isis was closely connected with Hathor whose physical attributes, the cow's horns and sun-disc, she adopted. The ancient Egyptians regarded the goddess as the 'eye of Re', although Plutarch conceived of her as a moon goddess. In Greek times Isis became the protectrix of seamen and received a rudder as one of her attributes as Isis Pharia.

Blood of Isis This sign, called tet by the Egyptians, resembles the ankh, except that the transverse arms are folded downwards. The blood of Isis is similar in many ways to the knot in the girdle worn by gods. Its original meaning is unknown, but after the New Kingdom the connection with Isis was unequivocal. In the Book of the Dead the sign was addressed with the words, 'O, blood of Isis'. It was placed with the deceased in the tomb and was supposed to be made of a red, semi-precious stone. The blood of Isis was often combined with the djed-pillar, especially in the decoration of temple walls, beds and sarcophagi. When combined, the two symbols alluded, via Isis and Osiris, to the unity of opposing world forces and with that to the unconquerable nature of life.

Iuwen The iuwen, the name of which means 'pillar', was an ancient fetish of the city of Heliopolis. It was raised up in a solemn ritual and a bull's head was often placed on top. As a pendant to an obelisk, the pillar became a lunar symbol. Osiris received the name Iuwen in his aspect of moon-god.

The tet symbol of the **Blood of Isis** was also the knot in the girdle of Isis and a powerful amulet of protection.

J

Jackal The term 'jackal' is not entirely justified from a zoological point of view but it has nevertheless been retained to describe the animal form of certain deities. The Greeks saw Wepwawet as a wolf and Anubis as a dog. The latter could have been a desert-dwelling wild dog, perhaps a cross with a wolf or jackal. Among many peoples canines became animals symbolic of death and guides in the netherworld because dogs were seen to eat dead bodies. Khenty-Amentiu was the lord of the necropolis of Abydos. Anubis who appeared in mortuary reliefs in all ages was regarded in Ptolemaic times as a true psychopomp. *See also* ANUBIS.

K

Ka The ka was a term for the creative and preserving power of life. In ancient times it referred particularly to male potency, hence its phonetic resemblance to the word 'ka' meaning 'bull', but it had soon come to mean intellectual and spiritual power. The hieroglyph 'ka' with hands raised in a defensive attitude was a magical gesture designed to preserve the life of the wearer from evil forces. The *ka* was born with a person. Many representations show the god Khnum fashioning the child and its *ka* on a potter's wheel. The *ka* accompanied a person like a kind of double, but when the person died the *ka* lived on. 'To go to one's *ka*' meant 'to die', since the *ka* then left its mortal house and returned to its divine origin. The *ka* needed sustenance above all for its continued existence which was provided in concrete form as offerings or symbolically in the tomb paintings which the Egyptians regarded as no less effective. Because sustenance contributed to maintaining the life force, foods were also regarded as being imbued with *ka*, hence the fact that plural concept 'kau' meant 'food offerings'. Rep-

View into the 'Treasury' in the tomb of Tutankhamun. Guarding the entrance is a black painted wooden figure of a **Jackal** reclining on top of a pylon-shaped box mounted on poles so that it could be carried in procession. A fine linen shawl is draped around the figure. In the background can be seen the wooden canopic chest within which was the canopic box that held the viscera of the dead pharaoh. XVIII Dynasty, *c.* 1354 BC. Tomb no. 62 in the Valley of the Kings.

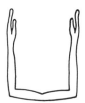

Two upraised arms symbolized the **Ka**, the double or 'doppel-gänger' that the god Khnum fashioned on his potter's wheel.

The ram-headed god **Khnum** of Elephantine fashions the young prince Amenhetep III on his potter's wheel, together with his *ka* or spirit double, whilst the goddess Hathor looks on and extends the ankh, sign of life. A series of reliefs in the temple at Luxor show the prince's mother being visited by the god Amun and the cycle of his birth and acceptance by the gods. These birth reliefs were copied from the similar earlier series in the temple of Queen Hatshepsut at Deir el-Bahari on the west bank of the Nile. Scenes of the creator god such as this appear frequently in the mammisi (birth houses) of the later periods, e.g. that of Nectanebo at the temple of Dendera.

resentations are known in which a 'ka' sign takes the place of food on the offering table.

Kamutef This word, references to which were made since the New Kingdom, means 'bull of his mother', and was an epithet of the ithyphallic Min and of Amun. The term characterizes the two gods as self-begotten entities who came into being without a father.

Khepresh *see* CROWNS

Khepri Khepri signifies the scarab as primeval god. He was 'he who came into being of himself', who appeared on earth without generation. In early times Khepri was already regarded as a manifestation of Atum and eventually he became equated with Re. The god in the form of a beetle rose from the netherworld as the morning sun, having been born from the womb, i.e. the eastern horizon, of his mother Nut, the sky. Khepri was also linked with the symbol of resurrection, as is stated, for example, in the Book of the Dead (Chap. 83), 'I have soared as the primeval one soars; I have become Khepri. I have grown as plants grow . . . I am the fruit of every god'. *See also* SCARAB.

Khnum Khnum was worshipped in the form of a ram into the early period of the New Kingdom but was then represented as a man with a ram's head. He was regarded at Elephantine as guardian of the source of the Nile who brought forth the inundation. His more important function was that of creator. Khnum fashioned the body of a child on a potter's wheel and implanted him as a seed in his mother's body. He also made the gods in that way. He was the 'father of fathers, the mother of mothers'. Together with Heket, the goddess of birth, he assisted at the birth. At Esna in southern Egypt Khnum was the creator of all beings, in fact he was the embodiment of the whole world. In him were united Re, the sun and heaven; Shu, the air; Osiris, the netherworld, and Geb, the earth. This explains the representation of Khnum with four heads. The god's name could mean the same as ram and denoted various ram heads who in historic times were to a large extent grouped together.

Khons The name of this Theban god means 'traveller', which referred to his traversing the sky for Khons was a moon god. He was represented as a young man in the form of a mummy with legs bound, bearing the moon's disc and crescent on his head. Because he was a divine child, his father being Amun and his mother Mut, Khons was connected with two other divine sons: with Shu who supported the sky and with the royal god, Horus. From the latter he derived the symbols of authority, the crook and flail. In allusion to the falcon god Horus, Khons often received a falcon's head whilst the moon-disc surmounting the moon-crescent became a sun-disc. The title 'Khons the child' is to be understood as a form of the young sun-god who was invoked as a protection against malevolent animals. In this aspect both Khons and Horus were shown in later periods standing on crocodiles. As Khons the adviser, called Chespisichis by the Greeks, he was called on to help in cases of illness. *See also* TRIAD.

King To the Egyptian the king was the centre of all existence. Because he was an entity both human and divine. He was the link between this world and the other. One Pyramid Text, (No. 1037), says of the king that 'there is no limb of mine devoid of God', which means that the king united all divine powers. The head corresponded to the Horus falcon, the face to the 'opener of the ways', the nose to Thoth, the thighs to the frog goddess and even the buttocks corresponded to Isis and Nephthys, which in the Pyramid Age had already been replaced by the day barque and night barque.

A relief in the temple of Amenhetep III at Luxor shows the god Amun assuming the form of the reigning king (Tuthmosis IV) and consorting with the queen (Mutemwia). Both are enthroned on the sign for heaven and the god holds the sign of life to the queen's nose. In a further scene the ram-headed creator god, Khnum, shapes the body of the future king (and his *ka*) who Amun has begotten. After the birth the mother goddess Hathor presents the child to Amun who greets it with the words, 'Welcome in peace, O son of my body'. This representation of the divine visit is based on an earlier version on the other side of the Nile in the temple of Queen Hatshepsut at Deir el-Bahari. Reliefs and paintings, for example, in the tomb of the noble Kenamun at Abd el-Qurna (Thebes), are well known, in which the feet of the young prince and future ruler rest upon a stool under which nine prisoners, symbolic of the nine traditional foreign peoples, lie bound in a crouched or kneeling attitude.

As son of Re the king was the sun-god's 'living image on earth'. He took symbolic possession of his property by performing the cult ceremony of 'running round the wall'. Besides the crook and flail, the symbol of earthly authority, he often carried the *was*-sceptre of the gods and his head was decorated with the uraeus, the fiery eye of the sun-god. Also part of the royal insignia was the animal's tail. According to one interpretation it was seen as a dog's tail once worn for hunting magic, but the Egyptians explained it as a bull's tail, since their king was regarded as 'mighty bull'.

Knife Knives used in ritual were supposed to be made not of metal worked by human hand but of flint. The twenty-second nome bore the name 'knife of flint'. The knife was a magic weapon, a symbol of defence for rendering evil things harmless, hence the fact that the hieroglyphic sign for the ass, a Sethian animal, was transfixed between the shoulders with a knife, to exorcise its harmful influence. According to the creation myth of Hermopolis, the birthplace of Re and the primeval hill lay in the middle of the 'lake with the two knives'. The two knives probably stood for the twin sycamores, which are mentioned elsewhere, between which the sun emerged on the horizon. They were represented as knives, because they alluded to the victorious battle of the sun-god with the powers of the netherworld, who wanted to hinder him at sunrise. Several vignettes in the Book of the Dead show a male cat, the deputy of Re, stabbing the Apophis serpent, the symbol of darkness. The knife was often also an attribute of the hippopotamus goddess Taweret. In myth the crescent moon was interpreted as a knife; therefore, an ancient text in which Khons the moon-god kills sacrifices for the king is to be understood in this way. Thoth decapitated evildoers using the crescent moon as a weapon.

Knot The knot was closely connected with the magic of binding and releasing. The knot held magic power fast. Amulets were often tied to knotted cords. The blood of Isis, an imitation of the knot of her girdle, was a popular amulet. The power inherent in the knot appears in Chapter 42 of the Book of the Dead (Budge 1928, 176) as a symbol of the hidden force of germination which grows anew motivated by its divine power of the beginning: 'I am the knot of the god within the *Aser* tree, and my going forth is the going forth of Re on this day'.

L

Ladder of heaven   The ladder of heaven was a familiar concept in the Pyramid Texts. It was repeatedly visualized in the sun's rays and therefore was under the charge of Re. In other cases it was viewed as a rope ladder or a stout ladder the uprights of which could be represented as djed-pillars, which belonged to Osirian symbolism. The ladder was intended for Osiris the god of resurrection and ascension. Osiris himself then became the symbol of the ladder of heaven for the believer. The Pyramid Texts speak also of a ladder with rungs formed from the arms of gods on which the deceased climbed up to heaven. According to the Book of the Dead (Chap. 98) 'the spirits of light' stand 'to both sides of the ladder of heaven'. Among other things the image of a ladder was placed with the deceased in the tomb.

Lapis lazuli   In the eastern Mediterranean this blue precious stone with speckles of gold, which is often erroneously called sapphire, was an image of the starry firmament. To the Egyptian it was also a sacred stone, the blue colour of which was an indication of its celestial origin – blue was the colour of the gods, especially Amun. Regalia were manufactured of gold and lapis lazuli in order to place the wearer under the protection of the sun and of heaven. Egyptian judges wore this stone around the neck inscribed with the word 'truth'.

There appears to be no natural source of lapis lazuli in Egypt, the nearest known is at Badakshan in north-east Afghanistan, which implies long trading routes at an early date since the stone was used in Egypt from predynastic times.

Leopard, panther   The goddess Mafdet was worshipped in the form of the leopard. She was the mistress of punishment but also a helper of the deceased. In ancient times the priests who presided over the Opening of the Mouth ceremony wore a panther skin. Stelae show the transfigured dead in panther skins receiving oblation. A panther skin was often depicted on coffin lids up to the Middle Kingdom. It is very likely that similar customs among African peoples were related to those of the ancient Egyptians, for the members of one northern Nigerian tribe bury their dead in leopard skins whilst in Loango the prince's hearse was hung with leopard skins. Among the Shilluk the dead ruler was also adorned with a leopard skin. The Egyptians may have thought of this in connection with some death-defying power, with its origin possibly in an age when animal skins were used as clothing. Figurines of panthers carved in wood, found in the kings' tombs of the Eighteenth Dynasty, carried statuettes of the king on their backs, as those from the tomb of Tutankhamun. The images of panthers which New Kingdom rulers wore on their belts may have had an amuletic character.

Lettuce   The lettuce was one of the most important attributes of the god of fertility, Min. A small bed of lettuce was carried in procession at the god's festival. The lettuce was shown in many reliefs of Min, and also in special depictions of Amun, as in the temple of Luxor, which identified him with Min. The plant was regarded as an aphrodisiac, which explains its popularity as an offering, since to maintain sexual potency meant to preserve live.

Light   With the Egyptians, as with other peoples, light was a divine function on account of its apotropaic power. Lights were lit in the temples on the night of the New Year. Plutarch speaks of an eternal flame with regard to the lights which were kept burning before the divine image. Light became a symbol of purity and goodness because it dispelled darkness and, therefore, averted typhonic forces. The task of the god Thoth was to protect the light from the darkness for, as 'representative of Re', he accompanied the sun-god on his daily journey and lit up the firmament at night as the moon. The mythical battle between light and darkness culminated in the injury and theft of the lunar eye (the waning of the full moon) which Thoth brought back and healed. Depictions of the Late Period show Thoth, in the form of a baboon with the eye in his hands, a symbolic expression for the return of the light. A flame was awarded to the deceased to light his way. The Book of the Dead (Chap. 137) tells of the shining eye of Horus which destroyed Seth's three-fold might and then animated the outcast as the 'fire of rebirth'. Elsewhere the fire spirit speaks the truly prophetic works, 'thanks to my light the mountains populated with tombs awake to the light'.

Lion In Egypt as in Mesopotamia, the lion was a solar animal. To begin with images of felines were only symbolic of the sun-god. In the Book of the Dead (Chap. 62) the text runs 'I am the Lion, Re'. In the New Kingdom the lion was regularly regarded as a manifestation of the sun-god, for the leonine deity Miysis was depicted with the sun-disc and in Hellenistic times received the epithets 'Re, light, fire, flame'. Under the name Herakhty, Horus assumed a lion's head as god of the morning sun. Since it was a solar animal the lion could symbolize not only destruction and death at night but also rebirth in the morning, hence the bier on which the mummy was laid was often given leonine form or feline feet. Most leonine deities were female. Above all there was the warlike Sekhmet who was equated with Bastet and with the Theban Mut. The lioness deity Mehit was worshipped in This and was often identified with the fire-spitting uraeus, the eye of Re. In Leontopolis a double lion god, Ruty, was venerated. He had already been equated in early times with Shu and Tefnut and his task was to watch over offerings to the dead.

The lion evokes widespread terror, therefore, he received apotropaic significance becoming the guardian of temple gateways and of the royal throne, hence its carving with the lion's legs and tail. Water spouts on temple roofs had the form of lions and were thus supposed to keep the power of Seth, which hurtled down in storms, away from the holy place. The god Aker, with two lion-heads, stood at the entrance to the netherworld. In the Archaic Period the lion as a symbol of strength had already become an image of the king. Ramesses II was once called 'the strong lion with raised talons and mighty roar, at whose voice the desert animals tremble'. The sphinx is known to have originated from the image of the lion.

Lotus Waterlilies shut their flowers at eventide and retreat so far into the water that they cannot be reached by hand. At daybreak, orientated to the east, they strive upwards again and open in the light. In myth the red waterlily, the lotus, 'the blossom which came into being in the beginning'

Red granite **Lion**, one of a pair dating from the reign of Amenhetep III (1417–1379 BC). This one carries an inscription recording its repair by Tutankhamun, *c.* 1360 BC. The reclining ease of the beast and the easy pose of the right paw dangled over the left show the sculptor's confident treatment of his subject in this hard stone. Both lions were originally removed to the temple at Gebel Barkal at the Fourth Cataract by a later Nubian king. (*See also* AKER.) British Museum.

appeared from Nun, the primeval waters, or 'emerged from the light'. This flower was close to both water and fire, to the darkness of chaos and the divine light respectively. The lotus emerging from the water became the symbol of the sun breaking forth after the night. A familiar concept to the Egyptians was that of the sun-god appearing on a lotus flower from the primeval lake. In Chapter 15 of the Book of the Dead Re appears as 'the golden youth, who came forth from the lotus'. In the same book (Chap. 81) the deceased utters the desire to be transformed into a sacred lotus, which is an expression of the hope of rebirth. The blue lotus especially was regarded as a sacred flower. In many New Kingdom tomb paintings one sees the deceased refreshing themselves with their fragrance. A wooden and painted portrait head of Tutankhamun from his tomb shows the king rising from a lotus blossom. The lotus was above all the plant belonging to the god Nefertem.

M

The goddess **Maat**, wearing her distinguishing feather on her head, embraces Seti I and extends the breath of life to him via the ankh which she holds to his nostrils. XIX Dynasty, *c.* 1310 BC. Tomb of Seti I, no. 17 in the Valley of the Kings, Thebes.

The symbol of the goddess **Mafdet**, the pole, rope and blade of execution, with the goddess represented in feline form running up it.

Maat The goddess Maat was the personification of the basic laws of all existence; she embodied the concepts of law, truth and world order. The most ancient hieroglyphic character probably depicted the straightness of the plinth on which the throne rested, which was also a symbolic representation of the primeval hill. The transfer of a physical concept to the field of ethics has its parallel in the English adjective 'straight' meaning 'honest', 'upright and true'.

Without Maat life was impossible for she was Re's food and drink. The seated image of this goddess, who wore an ostrich feather on her head, was held in Pharaoh's hand like a doll and was presented as an offering to the gods. This meant that the king was the representative of divine order. Judges were regarded as priests of Maat. In the Hall of Judgement at the Weighing of the Heart the heart of the deceased was placed on the scales of justice balanced against the feather of Maat, symbol of truth. Mention was often made of two Maat goddesses who were equated with the two solar barques, called Maaty.

Mace The round-headed mace, a royal attribute, was regarded as the seat of the supernatural power of the bearer. The royal god, Horus, was 'lord of the mace in order to smite down his enemies'. The symbol of power, the divine mace was kept in the inner sanctuary. The mace and the bow were attributes of the god Wepwawet. The mace was also a metaphor for the 'sound eye of Horus'. The king smiting his enemies with the mace is represented again and again on temple pylons. An inscription of Amenhetep II records him using the mace to smite rebellious princes in the presence of the god Amun. Since the mace consisted for a long time of white limestone, its picture was employed as the ideogram for 'white'.

Mafdet The goddess Mafdet, who was often venerated in the earliest times, was a manifestation of judicial authority and, above all, of the device used for execution. This consisted of a pole, curved at the top with a coil of rope round the shaft and a projecting blade. In pictorial representations Mafdet, in the form of a feline predator, runs up the pole. The goddess' claws were likened to the spear of Horus. Mafdet, however, did not only wreak terror on evildoers but also fought snakes. In representations from the Late New Kingdom she appears in scenes of the judgment hall of the beyond.

Malachite Malachite is green; hence it could express joy. The goddess of love, dance, music and joy, Hathor, was also entitled 'lady of the malachite' (and 'lady of the turquoise'). The eternal and freshly verdant 'field of malachite' was one of the dwelling places of the blessed along with Sekhet-Iaru, 'the field of reeds'.

Menat At first the menat was a piece of symbolic jewellery. It consisted of a broad necklace with several rows of beads gathered into a long counterpoise. As an attribute of Hathor it was imbued with divine powers of healing. A late temple relief at Dendera shows the goddess handing her menat to the king. Hathor herself bore the epithet 'great menat'. During the ceremonial dances the menat was used as a percussion instrument. From the times of the Ramessides it was placed with the deceased in the tomb as an amulet. Hathor's small son, Ihy, often carried the menat in his hands along with the sistrum.

The **Menat**, a broad necklace or collar, had a counterpoise hanging down behind it. Here a priestess of the goddess Hathor holds a Hathor-headed sistrum in her right hand whilst she offers her menat with her left.

Sandstone block from a dismantled temple of Queen Hatshepsut (1503–1482 BC) at Karnak. The queen is shown dressed as pharaoh wearing the White Crown and holding a vase in each hand dancing before an ithyphalic representation of the god **Min**. Other symbols of Min are (opposite, top to bottom): his fetish; the sign for the ninth nome of Upper Egypt; a round hut, and lettuce leaves.

Mertseger The Valley of the Kings on the west bank of the Nile at Thebes (modern Luxor) lies in the shadow of a naturally pyramid-shaped hill known as the 'Lady of the Peak'. The goddess of this area was Mertseger 'She who loves silence', and she was particularly worshipped by the necropolis workmen. She presided over the whole Theban necropolis and is usually represented as a snake goddess, a uraeus with a woman's head, or sometimes as a scorpion with a female head.

Meshkhent A goddess of birth who was identified with the brick upon which a mother squatted to give birth. She is often shown as a brick with a woman's head, or as a woman with a brick on her head. *See also* BIRTH BRICK.

Methyer The goddess Methyer was the embodiment of the primeval waters who, in the form of a cow, brought the sun-god into the world and raised him up to heaven between her horns. Plutarch has handed the name down as an epithet of Isis.

Milk Texts and paintings illustrate the king being suckled by a goddess, e.g. Isis, which parallels a symbolic rite whereby the ruler partook of divine powers. Other representations show the king drinking milk from the udder of the celestial cow, as in a relief from the temple of Dendera. Two pots of milk were often placed in temples as offerings. Milk was a metaphor for purity because of its whiteness, therefore offering milk libations could often be interpreted as a rite of purification. Vessels full of milk were placed with the deceased in the tomb; in this connection one Pyramid Text reads, 'take the breast of your mother, Isis'. This thought was later consciously altered to comply with Osirian symbolism; through this divine drink the continued existence of the god whom Seth had murdered was assured. Osiris' tomb had 365 offering tables on which the milk was not allowed to run out.

Min In earlier times this god was worshipped as a fetish, rather like a barbed arrow. This has been interpreted as various things from a lightning bolt to the union of man and woman. The god's emblem remained in altered form in the writing of his name and is also recognizable in the sign of the ninth Upper Egyptian nome. Min was a god of fertility, represented in human form, and his attributes were the following: legs placed tight together like those of a mummy, erect phallus, a flail above his arm which was raised stiffly with hand extended to one side, a skullcap on his head with two lofty plumes and two streamers hanging down the back. Others of his attributes were a bed of lettuce (an aphrodisiac), a round hut before which were bull's horns tied to a pole, and a small shrine surmounted by a leaf-shaped flabellum surrounded by lettuces. The round hut and the naos could be references to an ancient sanctuary of Min. Min moved from being the lord of fertility in animals to that of god of vegetation. His chief celebration was the so-called 'festival of the staircase' at which the god on his 'staircase' received at the king's hand the first ears of corn that had been harvested. The staircase may have been a stretcher for the divine image, or a threshing floor.

Mirror Mirrors always retained more or less the same shape, a flat, oval plate of polished copper with a wooden or bone handle. Since the Middle Kingdom at least, the sun-disc provided a model for the mirror. Some goddesses, for example, Hathor and Mut, were presented with two mirrors as a cultic offering.

Mnevis bull One of the several sacred bulls of Egypt. He was kept at Heliopolis, the centre of the early sun cult, and is represented with the solar disc and uraeus between his horns. As part of the sun cult he was regarded as an incarnation of Re and a mediator of the god Atum. One of the boundary stelae erected by Akhenaten in the fourth year of his reign at the edges of his new capital Akhetaten (Amarna) mentions arrangements being made for the worship of the Mnevis bull at Amarna. *See also* APIS; BUCHIS; BULLS.

Month, Montu This falcon-headed deity, who was originally worshipped in Hermonthis, was brought by the rulers of the Eleventh Dynasty to Thebes, where his significance as a royal god soon decreased in favour of Amun. There is still a small temple of Month in Karnak to the north of the great temple of Amun. The god was represented with a falcon's head surmounted by the solar disc and two tall plumes. He fought the enemies of the gods and made kings victorious, hence his character as god of war. He slew the opponents of his father Re with a spear, in fact he was equated in theology with the sun-god. The sacred animal of Month was a white bull with a black face who was called Buchis in later times. When animal

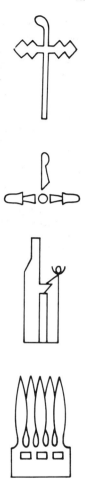

cults began to flourish this bull was increasingly regarded as an earthly manifestation of the god, and was buried at death with full ceremony. The burial places of the sacred bulls, the Bucheum, was found at Armant (Hermonthis) in 1927.

Moon The moon was regarded as the 'sun shining at night', therefore conceptions relating to the course of the sun were transferred to a lunar context. Because of this the moon may, for example, be adored by baboons or accompanied at night by jackals. Usually it was depicted as a disc resting on a crescent. The moon god Khons wore the disc and crescent as a head-dress. The sickle moon could be symbolized by a cutting weapon, like that which the moon god Thoth held in his hand, or by a leg which became a relic of Osiris. The phases of the moon were a symbol of life and death, alluding to the death and resurrection of Osiris. The fourteen pieces of Osiris' dismembered body corresponded to the fourteen days of the waning moon. The identification of the moon with the injured eye of Horus played a significant rôle in myth. In Hellenic times the goddess Isis, whom the Greeks saw as Selene, took a place alongside the more ancient moon deities, Thoth, Khons, Osiris and Iah, who in the few representations we have of him was shown as a man wearing the royal kilt with the moon disc on his head.

Eye of the Moon From early times the moon was regarded as the left eye of the sky god and was denoted in historical times by the eye of Horus. The waxing and waning of the moon probably gave impetus to the myth of the battle between Horus and Seth, the representatives of light and darkness. In the end Seth succeeded in stealing the eye of Horus and devouring it, which symbolized the disappearance of the moon. Then Horus with the help of other gods himself ripped out the eye of his enemy, or according to another version disembowelled Seth. It was also related that the eye of the moon had sunk into the waters of the celestial ocean and that Thoth and Shu retrieved it in a net. The myth of the eye of the moon had many points of contact with that of the eye of the sun.

Mountains Rocks and mountain summits were nearer to the gods. In the seventeenth Upper Egyptian nome people invoked the 'peak of Amun' in their prayers. In western Thebes, on the highest ridge of the desert mountains, was a temple dedicated to Thoth

and his baboons. Gods were called 'lords of the mountains'. In the netherworld was a 'great mountain above which the starry sky stretches. Its length is 300 leagues and its breadth 230 and the serpent who dwells therein is of 70 cubits'. The concept of a universal mountain also existed which the Egyptians, however, imagined as being split into a western mountain, called Manu, and an eastern mountain, called Bakhau. Both served as supports for heaven. According to one Pyramid Text (No. 390), the dead king was led up a 'ladder' to the 'great throne' on the mountain. The mountain range to the west of the Nile was the entrance into the netherworld. This was the province of Hathor, Lady of the necropolis. The mountainous country was desert to the Egyptian, hence the hieroglyph used for this, which was three rounded hills separated by clefts, also served as the determinative for 'cemetery', 'quarry' and the names of foreign countries.

Mourning Since the Old Kingdom the deceased was accompanied on the way to burial by two mourning women, one at his head and the other at his feet. They represented on an earthly plane the goddesses Isis and Nephthys bewailing the dead Osiris. While the men rarely or never showed their sorrow, female relatives usually had dishevelled hair and a dress torn open at the breast when lamenting the dead. The signs of mourning were the same as in other parts of the East. People scattered dust on their heads and beat their breasts. The Pyramid Texts describe the lamentation for Osiris. 'They beat their flesh for you, they smite their hands for you, they dishevel their hair.' Blue was occasionally the prescribed colour for mourning dress.

Mouth, Ceremony of the Opening *see* OPENING OF THE MOUTH

Mut The figure of the Theban goddess Mut can only be traced back to the Middle Kingdom but she might well have been worshipped before. She was usually represented as a woman with a vulture skin on her head, often surmounted by the Upper Egyptian crown which was certainly an attribute deriving from the days of Theban hegemony. She was regarded as the wife of Amun and their son was Khons. When Amun was exalted to the position of sun-god, Mut became the eye of Re and because the eye of the sun was manifested above all in leonine goddesses, Mut received the form of a lioness. In the Late

New Kingdom Mut assumed the position of a primeval deity and was then seen as the 'mother of the sun in whom he rises'.

Myrrh, myrrh tree Myrrh trees which grew in Punt, God's Land, were sacred to Hathor in so far as she was the mistress of fragrance and was regarded as 'lady of Punt'. In the Coffin Texts the deceased wishes that he might receive a meal under the myrrh trees near to Hathor. Myrrh was used for anointing, i.e. for purification. The mouth and lips of the deceased were anointed with myrrh that they might be pure for the enjoyment of the sacrificial food. Hathor herself anointed the dead that he might live in the west like Re and eat at his offering table. Numerous tomb paintings of the New Kingdom show the cake of unguent consisting of fragrant resin on the head of the deceased.

Detail from the wall-painting in the tomb of Rahmose showing women **Mourning**. They wear blue dresses and are professional mourners hired for the occasion, rather than relatives. XVIII Dynasty, *c.* 1379 BC. Tomb no. 55, Sheik 'Abd el-Qurna, Thebes.

Name A name contained its owner's whole being. People and objects actually only had an existence from the moment that they bore a name, therefore the name was more than a mere means of identification, for it signified the manifestation of an entity or the realization of a quality, hence the fact that it is said of Osiris, 'he purifies the lands in his name of Sokar; the fear of him is great in his name of Osiris, he endures unto the ends of eternity in his name Wennefer'. In the Book of the Dead (Chap. 142), Osiris has a hundred names, which in his case and that of other deities are a symbol of the profundity of the divine nature. One often finds an aversion to pronouncing the god's name, thus pseudonyms came into being as, for example, in the case of Herybakef, i.e. 'he who is below his moringa tree'. The true name of the god was 'hidden'. In the Pyramid Texts (Nos. 276 and 394) one god is mentioned 'whose name is unknown' and another deity whose name 'not even his mother knew'.

The life of each person was sustained by the secret powers of his name. One Egyptian proverb runs thus: 'whosoever's name is uttered, he then lives', hence the names of kings and dignitaries were repeatedly written on monuments and in inscriptions in order to ensure the survival after death of their owners. The direst punishment therefore was to obliterate the name either by execration or hacking it out of monuments. The 'heretic king', Akhenaten, was supposed to have been deprived of continued existence by the loss of his name. The only person who could curse or even destroy demonic powers was one who knew their names. The spirits of the next world were supposed to be rendered harmless with the words, 'I know you and I know your names'.

Naos   The term 'naos' refers to the shrine of a god, a kind of tabernacle on which the image of the god or his sacred symbol was set up. The majority of shrines were made of wood, since they were carried in procession on the divine barque. In a temple the naos had its own room, a chapel. In the mortuary temple of Seti I at Abydos there are seven chapels each dedicated to a god: Seti I as a god incarnate, Ptah, Herakhty, Amun, Osiris, Isis and Horus; the naos, placed on the divine barque, stood at the back of each room. The sides of gods' shrines were often adorned with figures of the king supporting the canopy. The naos was, therefore, an image of heaven; when the door of the shrine was opened, the rite was introduced with the words 'the gates of heaven are opened'.

National shrine   There were actually two national shrines, which were the symbolic representations of Upper and Lower Egypt and look back to the time of the prehistoric shrines of Buto and Hierakonpolis. It is possible that these referred originally to the two kingdoms. Ancient representations on cylinder seals show that the Upper Egyptian national shrine (called 'great house') imitated the form of an animal with horns and tail. The Lower Egyptian national shrine is likely to have been a simple hut of woven reeds. A more recent interpretation sees both as having been originally a hunter's trap and draws parallels with the Babylonian monster Tiamat and the fish which devoured Jonah. The hunter's trap was the abyss of the netherworld and whosoever entered it, perhaps as an initiate, would emerge again and live on. In historic times national shrines, also called chapels, were not permanent buildings but were only erected from time to time for ceremonial purposes. *See also* NEKHBET; WADJET.

Nefertem   Nefertem's form was that of the divine lotus. When represented anth-

Painted wooden portrait head of Tutankhamun as a young boy emerging from a lotus flower as **Nefertem**. XVIII Dynasty, *c*. 1354 BC. From the tomb of Tutankhamun, no. 62 in the Valley of the Kings, Thebes. Egyptian Museum, Cairo.

ropomorphically he wore it on his head often with the addition of two vertical plumes. In one Pyramid Text (No. 266) he was called the 'lotus-bloom which is at the nose of Re'; an apt description of his function as god of fragrance. Because of the lotus flower's solar symbolism Nefertem moved into the sphere of solar divinities; he dwelled 'each day' with Re, and in fact he and the child of the sun, Horus, united to become a single entity. Nefertem was often represented with a lion's head or standing on a recumbent lion, a solar animal. *See also* LOTUS.

Neith The old local goddess of Sais was a warlike divinity, a fact which is proclaimed by her attributes, the bow, shield and arrows. The goddess of war also blessed the hunter's weapons. The practice of placing weapons around the coffin in ancient times could be connected with the goddess's protective function. Her close relationship with the crocodile god, Suchos, who was called her son, can be explained by the proximity of her cult centre to the Delta. In the New Kingdom she was regarded as the 'god's mother who bore Re', whereby she assumed the position of a primeval goddess who was neither male nor female. She was the first to 'create the seed of gods and men'. Neith was, furthermore, a mortuary goddess; in the Pyramid Texts (No. 606) she watched over Osiris' bier together with Isis, Nephthys and Selket. The deceased was meant to partake of her divine power by means of the mummy wrappings, for the bandages and shrouds were a gift of Neith, who was regarded as the patroness of weaving. The earlier proposal that her symbol was to be interpreted as a weaver's shuttle cannot definitely be verified.

Nekhbet The vulture goddess Nekhbet was worshipped in El Kab, the ancient Egyptian Nekheb, capital of the third Upper Egyptian nome. After El Kab joined with the neighbouring town of Hierakonpolis (the Egyptian Nekhen and the royal residence of Upper Egypt), Nekhbet assumed the position of a national goddess; she represented Upper Egypt whilst Lower Egypt was represented by the protective snake goddess, Wadjet of Buto. The animals of the two goddesses became the symbolic animals of the two halves of the country. The vulture and the snake became part of the royal insignia, especially as adornments for the head, in fact, they became embodiments of the two crowns. Because of this the vulture could herself become a snake, for example, the two

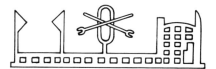

Symbols of the goddess **Neith**. On an ivory label from a I Dynasty tomb at Abydos is an early representation of a reed-built shrine dedicated to her with her standard outside. On a relief in the Ptolemaic temple at Dendera she is shown as a woman holding a tray of offerings and wearing her symbols of a shield and crossed arrows on her head.

The vulture goddess **Nekhbet**, together with her companion, the snake goddess Wadjet, symbolized 'The Two Ladies', protectors of the Two Lands. They are shown resting on two baskets. XII Dynasty. Detail from a processional shrine of Senusret I (1971–1928 BC) at Karnak.

uraei surrounding the solar disc were often interpreted as being Nekhbet and Wadjet. The two protective goddesses could appear as the mythical mothers of the king to whom they offered their breasts. Nekhbet was worshipped as goddess of childbirth in the popular religion of the New Kingdom and the Late Period. Her form was normally that of a woman wearing a vulture skin on her head, but in royal symbolism she often appeared in the shape of her sacred vulture. *See also* NATIONAL SHRINE; WADJET.

Nephthys One of the goddesses of the Ennead of Heliopolis, the sister of Isis and wife of Seth. She is sometimes said to be the mother of Anubis. Although married to Seth, her brother, she suffered none of the odium attached to his name in the mythology. She was a protector goddess of coffins and canopic jars, along with Isis, Neith and Selket. Often she and Isis are represented as a pair of hawks, their respective hieroglyphs on their heads, standing at either end of a bier on which lies the mummy of the deceased. Nephthys is found carved on the outer head end of royal New Kingdom sarcophagi kneeling on the hieroglyph for gold (Isis is at the foot). Later the two sisters occur painted together, often mourning, at the head end of sarcophagi of ordinary people. In scenes of the Hall of Judgement she stands with Isis behind their brother Osiris. She is much mentioned in the Pyramid Texts and the Book of the Dead but she does not appear to have been worshipped by herself or to have had her own cult centre.

Night In contrast to the darkness, which originated in primeval times, the night was a divinely created aspect of the world to which the powers of the unfathomable other world nevertheless had access. The darkness of night was at the same time a doorway to the mystery of existence. According to the Book of the Dead (Chap. 149) it was only possible to perceive the enigmatic Nile serpent by night. The writers of lamentations told how predators came out of their lairs at night and attacked men with illness and death. The impenetrable night also had positive, regenerative powers for as light broke through the darkness so life emerged from death. An illustration from the papyrus of Henuttawy expresses this hope of the Egyptians, for there 'death, the great god who made gods and men' is depicted as a fabulous animal with human legs, a snake's body with human head and a jackal-head at the end of the tail. Below the body a small sun sinks into the realm of night whilst the rising sun is held by two vulture's wings.

Nile *see* HAPI

Nomes, Nome signs Primitive images of nome gods, who were mostly in animal and to a lesser extent in plant form, or sacred objects usually served as nome signs. The provinces lying on the north-west edge of the Delta and the provinces in the south of Upper Egypt came into being at a later date, hence the fact that their nome signs are no longer on standards. The nomes were named after their symbols. As an example the Lower Egyptian nome signs have been illustrated here. The sign of the eighth Lower Egyptian nome attained special importance as a symbol of Osiris. In Egyptian temples the nome signs were depicted above anthropomorphic nome gods who personified their areas, the twenty-two Upper Egyptian nomes being on the south wall and the twenty Lower Egyptian nomes on the north wall. The latter are as follows:

1 'The white wall', i.e. the capital, Memphis. Beside the ideogram for 'wall' stands the character for 'white'.
2 'Thigh'. Capital, Letopolis. Originally the thigh of an ox brought as an offering.
3 'The western nome'. This nome sign is the ideogram for 'west', which is seen in other words but without the bird.
4 'Southern shield'. The shield of the goddess Neith with a stylized reed beside it which means south.
5 'Northern shield'. The papyrus plant refers to 'north'.
6 'Mountain bull'. The signs for 'mountain' and 'bull'.
7 'Western harpoon'. The sign for 'west' is beside the boat with the harpoon.
8 'Eastern harpoon'. The sign for 'east' is beside the boat with the harpoon.
9 'Anedjti'. The name of the nome god. Capital, Busiris.
10 Great black bull. Capital, Athribis.
11 'Heseb bull'.
12 'Cow with Calf'. Capital, Sebennytos.
13 'Name of uncertain meaning. Could be read both as 'Undamaged sceptre' and 'Ruler of Anedjti'. Capital, Heliopolis.
14 'The eastern nome'. Really 'the upper nome', since the sign for 'upper,' 'before' or 'foremost', which is a pot-stand, is next to the sign for east.
15 'Ibis'. Capital, Hermopolis.

Painting of the goddess **Nephthys** wearing her typical head-dress in the tomb of prince Amenhirkhopshef, a son of Ramesses III. XX Dynasty, c. 1190 BC. Tomb no. 55 in the Valley of the Queens, Thebes.

Dyad statue of the pharaoh Sahure accompanied by the god of the Koptos **Nome** wearing the nome sign on his head. V Dynasty, *c.* 2500 BC. Metropolitan Museum of Art, New York, Rogers Fund, 1918.

16 *'The fish'*. Capital, Mendes. The nome sign is the symbol for the Lepidotus fish. The nome-goddess was Hat-Mehit, who was represented with a fish on her head.

17 *'Behdet'*. The place of the throne. The nome sign is not represented here with its sacred object but with signs of the same phonetic value. These consist of *'bḥ'* (the tooth) with the *'d'* below and the *'t'* to the right above. Below the *'t'* is the sign for town, *niwt*.

18 *'Upper (Egyptian) royal child'*. Capital, Bubastis. The pot-stand is the sign for *'upper'*.

19 Lower (Egyptian) royal child. Capital, Tanis. The animal's rump means *'lower'*.

20 *'Sopdu'*. The name of the nome god whose sacred animal was a crouching falcon with a pair of erect feathers.

Numbers The number one alluded symbolically to the beginning, to the First Time which was regularly described as the era 'before two things had come into being in this land'. Two was an expression of duality and hence of the creation of up and down, day and night, man and woman. Among many peoples three is the all-embracing number; for example, the elementary relationship between father, mother and child was reflected on the divine plane; the Theban triad, Amun Mut and Khons, and the Osirian family with Isis and Horus are also cases in point. Prayers and oblations were given thrice daily because the day was divided into three parts, morning, noon and evening. Four symbolized attempts at spatial understanding. In the solar cult of Heliopolis four-sided altars were erected according to their orientation. The doubling of four created the ogdoad of Hermopolis, which consisted of four pairs of primeval deities.

The most important number in myth and magic was probably seven for this was the number of perfection. Re had seven *bas*, in fact, it was maintained that other individuals were sevenfold deities, for example, Hathor and Maat. The forty-two judges of the dead were really only a multiple of seven. The Egyptian saw the number nine as comprising the whole of humanity. The 'Nine Bows' symbolized the king's subject peoples. The term 'Ennead' denoted an all-embracing company of gods. The most important was that of Heliopolis to which Isis and Osiris also belonged. The universality of this concept is evident in the fact that there was also an Abydine 'Ennead' comprising seven gods and a Theban one comprising fifteen.

1. 9. 17.
2. 10. 18.
3. 11. 19.
4. 12. 20.
5. 13.
6. 14.
7. 15.
8. 16.

Signs of the twenty **Nomes** of Lower Egypt.

The sky goddess **Nut** extending herself in protection on the underside of the lid of the schist sarcophagus of the princess Ankhnesneferibre. The disc of the sun passes along the length of her body. The name of the princess in a cartouche can be seen above the goddess's left hand and elsewhere in the inscriptions. From Medinet Habu, Thebes. XXVI Dynasty, c. 525 BC. British Museum.

A thousand, the ideogram of which was the lotus, was a symbolic expression for a large amount and is often found in this sense in offering lists. The hieroglyphic for 100,000 was the tadpole which appeared in vast numbers in the Nile mud. The kneeling deity Heh was used to denote one million. He was often used on functional and decorative objects, as a symbolic figure for an endless span of years, i.e. eternity, and in this context he carried a palm leaf in each outstretched hand.

Nun *see* CREATION LEGENDS

Nut According to the Heliopolitan theology Nut was the daughter of the air god, Shu and sister of the earth god, Geb. She was the personification of the vault of heaven, which corresponded to depictions of her as a woman bending over the earth touching the western and eastern horizons with her hands and feet. She was the mistress of heavenly bodies which were all her children and of whom it was said 'they enter her mouth and emerge again from her womb'. Nut was therefore called 'the female pig who eats her piglets' and was variously represented as a suckling sow. She was also the mother of the sun-god Re, whom she swallowed in the evening and gave birth to again in the morning. Because she was connected to the symbolism of resurrection Nut played a part in funerary beliefs. The sarcophagus and the tomb chamber were decorated with stars or an image of the sky goddess, who often had vulture's wings or a small, round pot on her head. The coffin itself was the heavens, i.e. Nut from which the deceased awoke to new life.

Obelisk A sacred stone was worshipped in Heliopolis under the name 'benben' which was defined as the first manifestation of the primeval god Amun. The rays of the rising sun were supposed to have fallen on this stone first of all. The benben was the primeval form of all obelisks, which were monoliths, tapered towards the top and surmounted by a tip, called a pyramidion, which was probably gilded. These stone symbols were regarded as the dwelling place of the sun god. An obelisk stood in each Fifth

Dynasty sun sanctuary and before the temple pylons of the New Kingdom they were erected in pairs (*see also* PYLONS). This arrangement was probably adopted at first for reasons of symmetry but later it was expanded to include solar/lunar symbolism; the two stone columns were positioned in relation to the sun and moon thus uniting the poles of the cosmos within the sacred precinct of the temple. Gifts like bread and incense when used as offerings were shaped like an obelisk.

Offering table In prehistoric times an offering consisted of a loaf laid on a woven mat. This offering mat(*htp*) became the written sign for 'offering'. At the beginning of the Old Kingdom these mats were replaced by stone offering-tables which often imitated the hetep-sign in form or bore such a sign in relief on the top. The top of the hetep-sign, which corresponded to the loaf, always faced the person presenting the offering. Channels in the table were intended for libations. Often libation vases were outlined in relief on the tray. Offering tables which were recorded in text and picture were meant to maintain the offerings into eternity. Offering tables intended for the gods, in contrast to those set aside for the dead, had a hetep-sign on all four corners and together with the socle formed a kind of altar.

Ogdoad According to the Hermopolitan theology eight gods ruled before the creation of the world. These were the personifications of the primeval forces of chaos: Nun and Naunet, his wife, symbolizing the primeval waters; Heh and Hehet, the infinity of space; Kek and Keket, the darkness; and Amun and Amaunet, invisibility. As powers of the beginning of things they received the form of chthonic beasts; the male divinities were conceived of as frogs and the female as snakes. Sometimes the eight primeval gods were represented as apes greeting the rising sun; in this case the sunrise was thought to be symbolic of the creation of the world. Amun in his aspect of primeval god assumed the form of a snake and the name Kematef (called Kneph by Greek writers). The Ogdoad had a cult centre in western Thebes in the small temple at Medinet Habu.

Oil Oil which daily lessened pain and healed wounds was supposed to provide extensive power over this life when used in ritual anointing. It was said with regard to its use on the deceased that oil 'united the limbs,

joined the bones and assembled the flesh', hence preventing bodily decay which made existence in the next world ineffective. The offering liturgy in the mortuary cult included the presentation of seven oils besides the pouring out of water and censing. In a tomb painting at Deir el-Medineh (Tomb No. 2, of Kha 'Bekhnet) Isis and Nephthys stand at the bed of the deceased, one goddess holding the ankh and the other a vessel of oil. In one Pyramid Text (No. 451) holy oil was equated with the wedjat-eye. Glistening oil rendered the anointed immune from the powers of darkness.

Onuris (Anhur) The god of This in Upper Egypt. He was the divine huntsman, a sky god often identified with Shu. Representations show him as a bearded man holding a spear aloft in either one or both hands and wearing four tall plumes on his head.

Opening of the Mouth The rite of Opening the Mouth was supposed to return to the deceased the use of his senses by means of a magical act. The place where the ceremony was performed on statues was called the 'house of gold', i.e. the workshop of sculptors and goldsmiths. This animating magic was also performed on the corpse in the place of embalming. Although there are references to the Opening of the Mouth in the Pyramid Age, it is, nevertheless, only papyri dating from the Eighteenth Dynasty and later which are instructive with regard to the details.

After the preliminary rites of purification a bull was slaughtered, whose foreleg, the symbol of physical power, was extended towards the statue or mummy. Then the face was touched with various objects, among these one must make particular mention of the knife with a blade in the shape of a fish's tail, called *Peseshkef* and a hook-like device. Lastly, the statue was dressed and led to the sacrificial meal. This ceremony, which was also performed on divine images, was not only supposed to open the mouth but also to restore the other senses to life.
See illustration on p. 92

Orientation East and west were of outstanding significance because of the daily course of the sun. The concepts of birth and death were linked with these regions. The necropolis was usually placed to the west of the fertile land and the dead were euphemistically entitled 'westerners'. After the beginning of the Old Kingdom the dead were laid facing the rising sun. After the Fourth Dynasty the mortuary temple attached to the

The ceremony of the **Opening of the Mouth** being performed on the mummy of Hunefer. It stands before a stylized representation of the tomb, crowned with a small pyramid, and a stela inscribed with the name and titles of the deceased. A priest wearing a mask of the embalmer-god Anubis (an actual example of which survives in the museum at Hildesheim), supports the mummy before the mourners and other priests, one clad in the leopard skin of his office, perform the ceremony using the ritual implements. They included the foreleg of a sacrificed bull, a fish-tail flint knife, and a hooked implement. The ceremony ensured that the deceased would be able to answer questions put to him in the next world, especially those of the 42 gods who sat ranged in the Hall of Judgment where the heart of the dead person would be weighed on the scales as the questions were asked. Book of the Dead of Hunefer, XIX Dynasty, *c*. 1200 BC. British Museum.

pyramids was sited on the east face. The entrance to the pyramids was always on the north face, an orientation which alluded to the 'imperishable' circumpolar stars as an image of the next world. Not only tombs but also temples were orientated on an east–west axis although there are exceptions; the temple of Hathor at Dendera was aligned on the star Sothis, which was sacred to the goddess. The axis of the rock temple at Abu Simbel in Nubia was orientated directly towards the spot where the sun rose at the equinox.

Ornamentation   In ancient civilizations ornamentation often functioned not only as a decorative element but also with symbolic meaning. In Egypt, too, ornamentation cannot be attributed solely to an urge towards artistic style; it is far more a symbol and lifts the object, which conveys it into a higher realm. It is therefore to be expected that one would depict star decorations on ceilings, uraeus friezes high up on walls, and serried ranks of lotus flowers as in the primeval marsh near the floor because these corresponded to the symbolic comparison between the universe on the one hand and the temple, palace and, to some extent, the coffin on the other. The concept of the structure of cosmic order could be indicated in ornamentation. It is uncertain, however, how much this appertained, for example, to the spiral and looped motifs common in Egyptian tomb painting. When one sees interspersed rosettes or cows' heads bearing the solar disc, as, for example, on the ceiling of the tomb of Amenhetep III in the eastern Valley of the Kings at Thebes, one could be reminded of the sun's course. Various ornamentations contain pronounced symbolic motifs like the ankh, as in the tomb of Horemheb, or the djed-pillar, as in the tomb of Seti I, both in the Valley of the Kings at Thebes. It would, however, be wrong to interpret all ornamentation as symbolic. In later times its decorative character may well have been paramount.

Osiris   Osiris is the most well known figure in the Egyptian pantheon and probably possessed the most comprehensive symbolism. His name may mean 'place of the eye', and would therefore correspond to his written sign. In early times the chthonic fertility god, Osiris, had merged with Anedjti, the ancient royal god of Busiris. From the latter Osiris adopted the insignia of rule, the crook and flail. His vegetable aspect was symbolized by the corn; it was first trodden into the earth (burial), it then rested in the dark (the netherworld) and the new seed germinated (resurrection). It is understandable that a special relationship existed between life-giving water and the god, hence the Nile was called the 'efflux of Osiris'.

Osiris received earthly rule from his father, Geb. He introduced wine-growing and agriculture and received the name Wennefer, i.e. 'the eternally good being' or 'the perfect one'. His brother Seth envied his hegemony; he enticed Osiris into a chest and flung him into the Nile, thus the god's drowning, which symbolized the flooding of the fertile land, made a new harvest possible. The myth of the dismemberment of Osiris could have come about in a later age when several places maintained that they owned part of the god's body: Busiris possessed the back-bone (djed-pillar), Abydos the head, Mendes the phallus, Philae a leg. Each of these places had a tomb of Osiris which was usually on an island, thus consciously alluding to the primeval hill. A tree was planted close by the sarcophagus which was meant to imply that the god was risen from the dead. The major cult shrine of Osiris was at Abydos, where Seti I built a great temple in the Nineteenth Dynasty.

As ruler of the netherworld which he 'embraced' Osiris was the night form of the sun, in fact, people even wanted to see him as the moon, in connection with which the lunar phases were interpreted as being the death and resurrection of the god. The contact between the Osiris cult and that of Horus led to a juxtaposition of the two gods whereby the falcon deity was defined as the son of Osiris. From this the royal symbolism derived according to which the living ruler was the incarnation of Horus, whilst the dead king became Osiris. After the beginning of the Middle Kingdom all transfigured dead became Osiris who himself was a symbol of resurrection. The resurrection of Osiris was attributed partly to Anubis's art of embalming, partly to Isis who wafted the breath of life to the deceased by means of her wings, and also partly to Horus who embraced his father and gave him the eye of Horus to eat. The colour of the god's skin was symbolic; it was either white like mummy wrappings, black in illusion to the realm of the dead, or green as a token of resurrection. His feet were mostly close together in the attitude of a mummy.

A figure of **Osiris** seated before a desert mountain ridge dominates the end wall of the chamber in the tomb of Pashedu. Pashedu kneels in adoration behind the god's throne and above him is represented a wedjet-eye with hands that proffer two lighted tapers. Similar tapers in a vessel are held by a squatting geni in front of Osiris. A Horus-falcon looks on from the left. Tomb of Pashedu, XX Dynasty, 1186–1070 BC. Tomb no. 3 at Deir el-Medineh, Thebes.

Osiris bed   *see* CORN; CORN MUMMY

Osiris symbol The sign of the eighth Upper Egyptian nome with This as the seat of the royal residence, was a beehive-shaped structure surmounted by two feathers. Egyptologists interpreted the sign as the primeval hill which the name of the district, *Ta-Wer*, 'most ancient land' would seem to support. Fairly early the ancient Egyptians no longer understood the sign and henceforth it was connected with Osiris, being regarded as a reliquary for the god's head and correspondingly decorated with a head-band and uraeus. The town of Abydos, which likewise lay in the eighth nome, and supposedly owned the head of Osiris, adopted the nome sign with a minor alteration as a cult symbol. In the temple of Seti I at Abydos it is depicted several times as an Osiris symbol, sometimes on a portable framework, sometimes on a processional barque. In the Book of the Dead (Chap. 138) the symbol is found in the vignette accompanying the 'spell for the entry of the deceased to Abydos', where it often displays a small sun-disc between the plumes.

P

Palm A primitive representation of a date palm was already in evidence scored into Predynastic clay vessels used as grave goods. In Early Dynastic times a motif appeared of two giraffes flanking a tree. This tree cannot be identified with certainty but the animals seem to be eating palm branches. On the Fourth Dynasty seated statues of Khafre (Chephren), the sides of which are decorated with reliefs, are palm columns and papyrus stems representing the heraldic plants of Upper and Lower Egypt wound around the hieroglyphic sign for 'union'. Apart from her connection with the sycamore the goddess Hathor was called 'Lady of the date palm'. Either she or the sky goddess Nut handed food and drink to the deceased from a palm tree. The date palm was especially sacred to Re: with its tall trunk and ray-like crown of branches it was regarded as a place where the god manifested himself. This connection may also explain why the palm column, which derived from the date palm, appeared most commonly during the two periods in which sun worship flourished strongly – the Fifth

Dynasty, and under Amenhetep III and Akhenaten in the Eighteenth Dynasty.

The dom palm, which is especially recognizable by its double or triple trunk, was closely linked to Thoth, the god in baboon form, and to Min. Lastly, the general emblem of fertility was connected with the palm: in the tombs of the New Kingdom the dom palm adorns full granaries, which means that they are the embodiment of the divine giver of sustenance and of all herbage.

Palm leaf The palm leaf had symbolic significance as the sign for 'year'. A door in the temple of Medamud, now in the Egyptian Museum in Cairo, shows Senusret III receiving a palm branch, a token of a long reign, from Horus and Seth, respectively, the national gods of Upper and Lower Egypt. Occasionally a tadpole, the symbol for 100,000, was attached to the lower end of the palm leaf. In one relief on the outer wall of the first pylon at Medinet Habu, Amun, enthroned, hands the king a fourfold ideogram for heb-sed, a great jubilee celebration which was usually held for the first time after thirty regnal years, and was then repeated at shorter intervals. The palm leaf, worn on the head or held in the hand, was an attribute of the god Heh, the personification of eternity.

Panther *see* LEOPARD, PANTHER

Papyrus In art the papyrus plant was a symbol of the world which had arisen from the primeval waters. Papyrus columns supported the roofs of temples, in which the creation was daily repeated. Apart from this the papyrus was the heraldic plant of Lower Egypt and was dedicated to her goddess, Wadjet. The sign for Lower Egypt consisted of several papyrus stems growing from a tract of land. The ideogram of this umbelliferous plant meant 'green' and 'to become green' and it became a symbol for 'to flourish'. Wadjet, called 'the green', was often represented as a snake rearing up above papyrus clumps. In the Archaic Period the goddess had already received a papyrus stem as a sceptre. In the Old Kingdom this emblem was also assigned to Hathor and Bastet. Whole bunches of papyrus plants were handed to the gods and to the deceased for they signified triumph and joy.

Phallus Despite their advanced culture the ancient Egyptians adopted a more open view of natural urges and had a cleaner attitude to them than their successors the

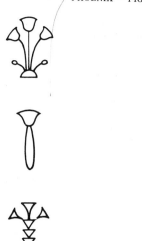

Three forms of **Papyrus**: representing Lower Egypt; a papyrus sceptre, and flowering papyrus.

Greeks and Romans. All erotic matters were handled in text and depiction with the utmost discretion. In places where sexuality acquired a significance over and above workaday affairs, it was represented with an almost childlike innocence but at the same time with extreme seriousness and was sublimated by being displayed through symbolism. The image of the vulva was used as the hieroglyphic sign for 'woman'; likewise, the phallus entered the written language as the biconsonantal sign '*mt*', as in the words for 'semen', 'poison' and 'midday'.

A decidedly symbolic meaning must have been attributed to ithyphallic representations, as in the case of the fertility god Min, and Amun when the latter was identified with him. This also applied in the end to the dead Osiris whose vital member was a symbol for life forces overcoming death. Numerous wood and stone models of phalli which were meant to be effective for conceiving children were found in front of the cult image of Hathor in the temple at Deir el-Bahari.

Phoenix The sacred bird of Heliopolis was at first probably only a wagtail, later a heron. With its long straight beak and head adorned at the back with two erect feathers it seemed to appear from the water like the sun. Its name, Bennu, Phoenix in Greek, was derived from the word *wbn*, i.e. 'to shine', 'to rise'. It enjoyed a cult alongside that of the sun-god, Re, in Heliopolis where it dwelt on the benben-stone (obelisk) or in the sacred willow. The phoenix was regarded as the *ba* of Re but was also a manifestation of Osiris. The deceased expressed the following wish, 'I have gone forth as a phoenix.' (Book of the Dead, Chap. 13). In the Late Period the hieroglyphic sign of the phoenix was used to denote Re. The phoenix was regarded as 'Lord of jubilees', which probably led to the conception of this miraculous bird's long life. According to Greek tradition the phoenix was a symbol of life renewing itself through a fiery death, which was an image of the sun rising at dawn.

Pig The ancient Egyptians regarded the pig as unclean as was later the case under Judaism and Islam. It was seen as the familiar of the evil god Seth. In the Book of the Dead (Chap. 112) the text states that Seth attacked the god Horus 'under the disguise of a black boar' and injured his eye or, according to another version, swallowed it. In the reliefs in the temple at Edfu Horus hunted Seth who was in the form of a pig. In the

95

The worker god of Memphis, **Ptah**, is generally represented as a standing, mummiform figure with hands protruding from the tight shroud to hold a sceptre that combines the *was* and djed-pillar symbols. He wears a tight-fitting cap, and has a menat hanging down behind his neck. This relief on the Ptolemaic temple at Kom Ombo shows him within a shrine topped by a frieze of royal uraei, and his name is inscribed in hieroglyphs before it.

'Book of the Gates' the judgment scene shows a ship above the steps leading up to Osiris in which a monkey is driving a pig before it as a symbol of evil.

The pig appeared in special relation to the moon; it was slaughtered at lunar festivals and presented to the moon-gods, Isis and Osiris. One myth relates how the sky goddess Nut assumed the form of a pig and devoured her own children, the stars; each evening, however, the young were reborn from the celestial sow. The sow with her piglets became a popular Egyptian amulet because she was a symbol of maternal fertility and the inexhaustible spring of life. It has remained a good luck token into modern times.

Primeval hill The appearance of the primeval hill from the primeval waters denoted the emergence of the world. The creator god rested on the primeval hill; in the Pyramid Texts, for example, No. 1587, Atum himself was addressed as 'hill'. The city of Memphis created its own personification of the primeval hill in the form of Ta-tjenen, i.e. 'the elevated land'. In Heliopolis the sacred Benben stone was equated with the primeval hill. Thebes later maintained that it possessed 'the glorious hill of the primeval beginning' and was, therefore, more ancient than any other town. In Osirian symbolism the primeval hill was interpreted as being the god's tomb. Tombs of Osiris which were set up in various places were usually situated on an island; the rise and fall of the water were supposed to allude to death and resurrection. *See also* CREATION LEGENDS.

Processions The purpose of religious processions was to make the gods' existence visible to all people. Whilst only the priests had access to the god in his sanctuary, laymen could then also view 'the beauty of their lord'. The real cult image was, however, hardly displayed to public view because it remained shut in the naos in the barque. Accompanying statues of gods were sometimes borne on a stretcher or a carrying-chair. The processional way was strewn with sand, a means of ritual purification. Often gods travelled considerable distances in a boat on the Nile as, for example, when Hathor of Dendera paid her annual visit to Horus of Edfu, a symbolic allusion to the union of the sky-goddess and the sun-god.

Pschent *see* CROWNS

Ptah The local god of Memphis was always represented in human form. He was wrapped like a mummy with a shaven head and tight fitting cap. His sceptre was a combination of the djed-pillar and the was-sceptre. To start with he was perhaps only a god of craftsmanship, therefore the invention of the arts were attributed to him, but in the Pyramid Age he had already assumed the position of a creator god. He created by means of his heart and tongue, thus fashioning the world by the power of his word. The god's creative power was then manifest in every heart-beat and in every sound. Ptah was regarded as 'the ancient one' who united in his person the entity Nun, the masculine aspect and Naunet, the female aspect. The people knew Ptah more intimately as the 'sculptor of the earth' who, like the god Khnum, created all beings on a potter's wheel. Ptah assimilated the nature of Osiris through his connection with the Memphite earth and mortuary deity, Sokar. He therefore in the Late Period became a composite deity, Ptah-Sokar-Osiris, represented as a standing mummiform figure like Osiris with tall plumes on his head. *See also* SOKAR.

Purification Without purification the effectiveness of ritual was called into question. Above the entrance to the temple the following text was often written: 'May he who enters the temple be pure'. Basins before the temple gateway were for ritual ablution. Priests and kings had to undergo ritual purification again and again. 'Water of all life

The **Pylons** that front the great temple at Luxor are characteristic of those of the New Kingdom and later built before all major temples. These are typical in having deep slots cut into them which once held the tall wooden staves from the top of which flew flags (the origin of the hieroglyph for god, *ntr*). Originally there were six statues of Ramesses II (1304–1237 BC) before the pylons, two seated and one standing on either side. Only one of his two obelisks that flanked the entrance remains, 82 ft high; its companion is in the Place de la Concorde, Paris. The earliest part of the temple lies back through the hypostyle hall that can be seen between the pylons. The temple was begun under Amenhetep III (1417–1379 BC) with a fine colonnade off which was the birth-room with the reliefs of him being fashioned by Khnum. Subsequent enlargement of the temple by later pharaohs elongated it to the north until Ramesses built the pylons seen here.

and well-being' was mentioned in connection with the king's bath; the royal bathroom, called the 'house of the morning', was always situated in front of the actual temple, as at Edfu, where it was built into the forecourt. The sun-god Re also purified himself in the celestial ocean before each daily voyage. In the Pyramid Texts a purificatory bath for the deceased is often mentioned whereby one was guaranteed not only cleanness but also new life. The purification in the initiation ceremony of the Isiac mysteries is mentioned by the classical author Apuleius. Baptism by sprinkling water can be traced back to the Egyptian custom of pouring water (lustration) over a person during the ritual bath.

Pylon Towers on either side of temple gateways are not in evidence until the New Kingdom. Their importance may have lain essentially in averting evil and anything hostile to the gods. Apart from this the two pylons were equated with the divine sisters Isis and Nephthys, who uplifted the sun which shone on the horizon. It is not definitely known whether the pylons were supposed to represent the two mountains between which the sun rose, but it is certain that the pylons which were linked with Isis and Nephthys were imagined as guardians of the god resting in his sanctuary.
See illustration on p. 97

Pyramid Pyramids can be traced back through architectural history to a development from step-shaped mastabas. An established plan for building pyramids was developed in the Fourth to Fifth Dynasties. The entrance corridor on the north face retained its orientation towards the circumpolar stars which were regarded as the 'imperishable ones' among which the deceased wished to dwell in the next world. The tomb chamber was sited facing west, the kingdom of the dead. The temple intended for the cult of the king lay on the east side of the pyramid where the sun rose. In the Middle Kingdom this arrangement was no longer strictly maintained.

The basic symbolic meaning of the pyramid could have been that it was the primeval hill rising from the waters of the beginning as in the case of simple tumuli and mastabas, which were rectangular flat-topped tombs of unbaked or baked brick. According to an Old Kingdom inscription the tip of the pyramid, which was gilded, came to be linked with the sun. The king who was buried in the pyramid entered into office

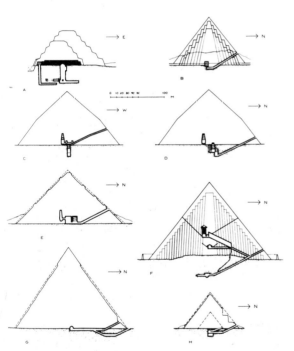

Cross-sections of the major **Pyramids** of the Old Kingdom, drawn to the same scale, and showing their development in shape and size. The major period of pyramid building was at the beginning of the IV Dynasty and within just over one hundred years. The pyramids here are: A Zoser, at Sakkara, III Dynasty, c. 2670 BC; B Huni (?), at Meydum, III Dynasty, c. 2613 BC; C, D Sneferu, Blunt or Bent Pyramid at Dahshur, IV Dynasty, c. 2600 BC; E Sneferu, North or Red Pyramid at Dahshur, IV Dynasty, c. 2590 BC; F Khufu (Cheops), Great Pyramid at Giza, IV Dynasty, c. 2560 BC; G Khafre (Chephren), at Giza, IV Dynasty, c. 2540 BC; H Menkaura (Mycerinus), at Giza, IV Dynasty, c. 2530 BC.

in the celestial beyond as the son of Re. In the New Kingdom small pyramids of stone were placed with the dead in the tomb, usually inscribed on the eastern side with a prayer of the deceased to the rising sun.

Pyramid Texts Their first occurrence is on the walls of the burial chamber and corridors of the pyramid of Unas at Sakkara. He was the last king of the Fifth Dynasty, died *c.* 2345 BC. They then appear in the pyramids of the Sixth Dynasty pharaohs and queens, after which date they tend to be appropriated for use by the nobles. Essentially the Pyramid Texts are a body of texts, spells, incantations or utterances designed to ensure the well being of the pharaoh in his next life in the sky with the gods. Faulkner (1969) lists a total of 759 utterances, comprising 2291 section numbers. No pyramid has produced a complete series of the texts, and many have variant versions of different utterances. They are the oldest corpus of Egyptian religious and funerary literature extant and, in many instances, are obviously much older than their first written occurrence. Many of the ideas expressed in them reach back into Predynastic times and reflect a tribal society.

Q

Qadesh A goddess of Syrian origin who was probably introduced into Egypt early in the New Kingdom. She was identified with Hathor as a goddess of love and is usually represented as a naked woman holding flowers standing facing the viewer on the back of a lion.

Qebsennuef *see* CANOPIC JARS

R

Ram Besides the bull, the ram was regarded as a symbol of fertility. At Elephantine and Esna it was worshipped as Khnum, at Herakleopolis as Herishef and in the region of Letopolis as Kherti. Amun could also appear in the form of a ram. The ram of Amun was distinguishable from the other sacred rams because the horns curved

The entrance passage and part of the wall of the burial chamber in the pyramid of Unas at Sakkara covered with the **Pyramid texts**. Many of the hieroglyphs of animals or birds that could cause harm were neutralized in the inscriptions by having their legs removed, or otherwise incapacitated. V Dynasty, *c.* 2345 BC.

Funerary stele with the Syrian goddess **Qadesh** standing on a lion and holding bunches of lotus and papyrus in her hands. On the left stands the ithyphallic god Min, and on the right the Syrian god of war and thunder, Reshef. From Thebes. XIX Dynasty, *c.* 1250 BC. British Museum.

downwards, whereas the others had horns projecting horizontally. These belonged to the indigenous breed, *ovis longpipes*, which was displaced from the Twelfth Dynasty onwards by the fat-tailed sheep, *ovis platyra*, which was the same breed as the ram of Amun. The ram worshipped at Mendes in the Delta, which had no particular name, was replaced by a billy-goat when that more ancient breed died out. In inscriptions of the Ramesside period it was said that Ptah slept with the queen in the form of the ram of Mendes. In the Middle Kingdom the ram of Mendes was described as the *ba*, i.e. soul, of Osiris and since he was also regarded at the same time as the 'life of Re, life of Shu and life of Geb' he became the embodiment of a cosmic quaternity, hence his image was that of a god 'with four heads on one neck'.

Re To begin with the sun god's name referred to the heavenly body itself. In early times Re already possessed a cult centre at On (the Greek Heliopolis, 'sun city'). He joined with Herakhty, i.e. Horus as the morning sun, and adopted from him the falcon head on his own human body. Because of a coalescence of Re and the creator god Atum, the latter became a manifestation of the setting sun. After Khafre of the Fourth Dynasty Egyptian kings termed themselves 'son of Re'. When Amun assumed the premier place in the pantheon in the Middle Kingdom, Re could not be suppressed, so the two deities consolidated their position by fusing into Amun-Re. The sun-god crossed the celestial ocean in his barque as helmsman of the world, accompanied by his vizier, Thoth, and his daughter, Maat, the embodiment of cosmic order. The sun was regarded as the visible 'body' of the lord of heaven but was also considered to be his eye. *See also* SOLAR BARQUE.

Red Red has a stronger effect on the senses than all other colours and among the ancient Egyptians it already symbolized life and victory. During celebrations the inhabitants of the Nile painted their bodies with red ochre and wore jewellery of red cornelian. Seth, who stood in the prow of the divine barque and stabbed the serpent of the netherworld, Apophis, with his lance was said to have had red eyes and red hair. Once the early defamation of Seth had set in red became an expression of danger. Red became a figurative expression for anger, a person 'with a red heart' was in a rage; 'to redden' meant the same as 'to die'. Red bulls were

sacrificed in the belief that the 'red god' was being destroyed. Red was also the colour of all-destructive fire. In the fifth hour of Amduat the lower region of Sokar's cavern was shown with red, wavy lines, in allusion to the 'lake of fire' in which the damned were punished.

Renenutet This name which characterized the nature of the goddess consisted of two parts: '*rnn*' (nourishment) and '*wtt*' (snake). Her epithets 'lady of the fertile land' and 'lady of granaries' denote her function as a goddess of fertility and harvest. During the gathering of corn and pressing of grapes people made offerings to her before her image which was in the form of a snake or possessed a snake's head. Representations of her exist in which she carried the still immature corn god, Nepri. Her concern was above all for the nourishment of children. The Greeks called the goddess Thermuthis. Graeco-Egyptian terracottas often show her as a form of Isis with a snake's head rising from a female body.

Reshef (Reshpu) A Syrian god of war and thunder invariably shown brandishing various weapons. He wears the White Crown of Upper Egypt, which has a streamer flowing from the top, and at the base of the crown above his forehead are the horns or a complete head of a gazelle.

Right — Left In Egypt the left was regarded as the side of death. According to the Ebers Papyrus (sixteenth century BC), the breath of life entered the body through the right ear but the breath of death through the left. When Horus seized the arm of the dead Osiris from his enemies (Book of the Dead, Chap. 1), that signified victory over the powers of death. The left eye of the lord of heaven corresponded to the moon and hence to night time, whilst the right eye was the sun and daytime. Right and left were also applied to the sexes as expressions of the polarity of world order; for men the right side was regarded as good and for women the left. The king was equated with the sun and the right eye, whilst the moon and the left eye were equated with the queen. The identification of the left side with the east and the right with the west is only an apparent contradiction to what has been said above concerning the sides belonging to life and death; the sun does indeed rise in the east and travel to its setting, i.e. to death, but when it sinks in the west this leads to rebirth.

Ring The symbolism of the ring lies in its roundness, for being without beginning or end it is a symbol of eternity. The hieroglyphic sign for 'eternity' was a ring which bore a certain similarity to a looped rope with the ends tied in a knot. Divine animals, for example, the hovering falcon in the temple of Horus at Edfu, often held this symbol of eternity in their claws. The bottom of the palm leaf, which Heh often held, terminated in the ring, representative of the cycle of eternity, as is seen on the back of the cedarwood chair from the tomb of Tutankhamun. In popular superstition magic rings were imagined to give protection from illness and other unpleasantness. Other knotted amulets were the ankh, the blood of Isis (tet), and the *sa*.

Road, path The Egyptians saw the path of the sun as having the most obvious allusion to his own path through life and, at the same time, he derived from it hope of his own survival after death. Like the sun-god the deceased had to withstand numerous dangers on his way through the netherworld. There were many books which were supposed to familiarize the deceased with the topographical features of the next world, for example, the 'Book of the Two Ways' from the start of the Middle Kingdom, and the 'Book of the Netherworld', Amduat, in the New Kingdom. The nightly journey of the sun was shown with hideous visions of gates of fire, demons and the serpent Apophis; this served as a comparison with the journey of mortals in the hereafter. The board game senet which means 'the way' was used as a symbol of the road leading through the netherworld. Walking a crooked path was to the Egyptian an image of passing through, of a transitional state. In this world, therefore, the road alluded to initiation but with regard to the hereafter it referred to the road whereupon the soul was cleansed.

Rope The rope and cord were generally images of bondage. On the Narmer palette the capture of the inhabitants of the papyrus land was shown by the falcon of Horus holding a rope in his claw standing on the sign for land which ends in a head on the left and has six papyrus stems on top. The god Onuris, the personification of the divine hunter, caught the enemies of Horus with a rope and killed them with his spear. In the ninth hour of the 'Book of the Gates' the enemies of Osiris appear bound with ropes, and in the tenth hour the opponent of the sun, Apophis, was fought with spear and rope. In pictures

The Syrian god **Reshef** standing in typical pose with upraised spear and shield wearing the White Crown with a gazelle's head on the front. Late Period, after 1000 BC. Metropolitan Museum of Art, New York.

The **Ring**, symbol of eternity, is often held by gods such as Heh.

A detail of the upper part of the limestone mace-head of king Scorpion shows small birds (lapwings, symbolic of the people of Lower Egypt), strung up by their necks on **Ropes** hanging from nome standards. Similarly roped captives are shown on the Narmer and bull palettes (pp. 18 and 35). From Hierakonpolis. I Dynasty, c. 3100 BC. Ashmolean Museum, Oxford.

The **Sa** is a symbol of protection; the hieroglyph represents a herdsman's rolled up shelter of papyrus.

and texts of the netherworld the rope could also be a symbol of fate. Gods and demons were themselves pulled by a rope as their ship was towed. The rope was sometimes replaced by a snake's body. Beings who determined fate were often termed 'surveyors of fields' and carried a rope rolled in a spiral. Time was part of fate. In the eleventh hour of the 'Book of the Gates' the rope was held by twelve goddesses of each hour who accompanied Re in his barque through heaven and the netherworld. Another representation showed twelve gods standing in the loops of a doubly twisted rope; these gods were called 'the bearers the one with double coils from whom the hours come forth'.

Sa   As a sign of magical protection the *sa* was the characteristic attribute of Bes figures and also of Taweret who was venerated as the goddess of childbirth. This sign of protection is also found as an independent symbol on magic wands of the Middle Kingdom.

Sacred animals   *see* ANIMALS

Sacred lake   The sight of the fertile land appearing each year from the waters of the inundation led to the concept of the primeval hill emerging from Nun, the primeval waters. The larger temples, therefore, possessed a sacred lake in which creation was imagined to renew itself each morning, a symbol for the beginning of the world. Several inscriptions describe the water of the sacred lake as the primeval waters in which the sun-god daily cleansed his face. Amenhetep III had a great stone scarab set up by the temple lake at Karnak as a symbol of the rising sun. The priests undertook their ritual bath in the water of the sacred lake and the deceased also desired to be purified there. Images of these lakes which functioned as libation bowls, are found on offering tables placed in the tomb of the deceased. Sacred lakes were mostly rectangular in imitation of the shape of artificial garden pools. The sacred lake at Heracleopolis was supposed to have come into being from the blood and discharges of Osiris or Herishef. In the 'Book of the Gates' a rectangular stretch of water was called 'the

'sea of life' on the edge of which stood twelve jackal-headed deities.

Sandals The foot as well as footwear were symbols of authority and of the acquisition of property. Pharaohs wore sandals with the pointed toe bent backwards and captured enemies were represented on the soles so that the king would symbolically tread on them. Sandals were a token of regal dignity. They were part of Tutankhamun's grave equipment, being kept in a wooden box with the following legend: 'the sandals of His Majesty, life, prosperity, health!' White sandals played a part in the mortuary cult as a symbol of purity, for the deceased approached Osiris wearing them having been freed of all earthly dust and dirt. In Ptolemaic times a pair of sandals was often painted on the lower end of the coffin, on the outside beneath the deceased's feet.

Sarcophagus, coffin The sarcophagus was the 'lord of life'. It was expected that the sarcophagus would grant eternal power which was made accessible to the deceased by means of symbols, magical pictures and spells recorded on the walls. The deceased was supposed to be able to leave the sarcophagus, i.e. his house, through a door painted inside the sarcophagus or on the

The **Sacred lake** was a necessary part of all large temples. Not only was it the place for the priests to undertake their purification, it was also used for ceremonies involving sailing the barque of the god or goddess of the temple to which it was attached. Here, at the Ptolemaic temple of Hathor at Dendera, it stands on the north side of the temple, and has a stairway for access at each corner. Around and behind it are the rubbish dumps of pottery enclosed within the great mud brick temenos wall.

Great granite **Scarab** set up on a plinth beside the sacred lake at Karnak, Thebes, by Amenhetep III (1417–1379 BC) and dedicated to Atum. This pharaoh is also known for a series of large commemorative scarabs issued during his reign referring to his marriage to Queen Tiy; digging a pleasure lake for her; the arrival of the princess Gilukhepa from Mitanni; his slaying of lions and of wild cattle. Other large scarabs were the heart scarabs, but most were small and carried the name and titles of their owner, or were amulets with a good luck inscriptions.

outer side. The pair of eyes depicted on the outside, or often on the inside from the Eighteenth Dynasty, provided a further link with the outside world.

In the Old Kingdom a strip inscribed with the name and titles of the deceased sufficed. In the Middle Kingdom vertical columns were added which were often dedicated to certain gods who would protect the deceased. These were Isis and Nephthys at the feet, and the four children of Horus at the corners of the side panels. In the New Kingdom images of divinites were placed next to the written signs. On the inside of the lid there was often a picture of the sky goddess Nut. The mummiform coffin became prevalent in the New Kingdom, probably because of identification of the deceased with Osiris. The feathered sarcophagi of the Tuthmoside period, which are covered by a pair of wings reaching from shoulder to feet, are a similar identification because Isis protected Osiris with her wings and wafted the breath of life towards him. The image of a vulture was placed on the breast of the deceased; its wings were adopted by the sky goddess Nut who was supposed to watch over the heart of the dead person. At the end of the New Kingdom solar symbolism came to the fore in the image of the winged disc or the beetle pushing the solar disc before it.

Satis   After the Middle Kingdom Satis was regarded as the 'lady of Elephantine', and as the wife of the creator god, Khnum. She was the giver of water which she presented to the deceased for purification (Pyramid Text No. 1116). Satis was depicted in human form wearing the Upper Egyptian crown on the side of which were two curved antelope horns. When Khnum was identified with Re, she became the 'eye of Re' whilst in allusion to Hathor, who was also regarded as the solar eye, she assumed the features of a goddess of women and love.

Scarab   The sacred beetle was an image of self-creation since the Egyptians believed that the beetle came into being of itself from a ball of dung, which in reality only serves to protect the eggs and larva. Thus the anthracite-coloured dung beetle was worshipped under the name Khepri, i.e. 'he who came forth from the earth'. He was already equated in early times with the creator god Atum and was regarded as a form of the sun-god. The beetle pushes a ball of dung before it, therefore, it was thought that Khepri rolled the solar ball across the sky.

The sun beetle, giving light and warmth, became a popular amulet in steatite or faience and was placed with the deceased in the tomb as a symbol of new life.

Scimitar Whoever wielded the sword was master over life and death, hence it was an attribute of several deities of the ancient east. A relief in the pillared hall of the temple at Abu Simbel shows Amun-Re handing Ramesses II the scimitar, symbol of strength. The victorious king had himself depicted brandishing the sword in his right hand, whilst his prisoners, symbolizing captive peoples, pleaded for mercy as he seized them by the hair with his other hand.

Scorpion As in the case of other dangerous animals the scorpion was accorded divine veneration. Seven scorpions were said to have helped Isis against her enemies. In the Archaic Period small figures of this animal were worn as an amulet. The goddess Selket, Selkis in Greek, was worshipped in the form of a scorpion. She was regarded as the protector of the living and the dead. She kept watch over the body of Osiris together with Neith, Isis and Nephthys. The four goddesses likewise protected the dead person's intestines and were, therefore, often represented on the canopic chest. Selket often wore the scorpion on her head as, for example, on the canopic chest of Tutankhamun and her standing figure that guarded it. *See also* SELKET.

Sea The primeval ocean, a sluggish, chaotic expanse of water, was the basic reality in all Egyptian cosmogonies out of which the world emerged, whether it was by the appearance of a primeval hill, the unfolding of a lotus flower, or by the hatching of an aquatic bird from an egg. The primeval waters were embodied by the god Nun whose temporal precedence was expressed in the title 'father of the gods'. The paternal aspect of the sea was, however, limited in myth to the passive rôle of a kind of cradle in which the actual creative force brought itself into being. According to the 'Book of the Heavenly Cow' the sun-god Re addresses Nun as 'O you, the eldest of the gods from whom I emerged'. All seas were only subsidiary parts of Nun from whom rainwater and the Nile floods also came.

Sekhem The word sekhem meant 'power' and also denoted those entities, for example, the stars, which stood between gods and men. The sekhem was also a divine charac-

The **Sekhem** sceptre was a symbol of power and authority. As such the hieroglyph was often used as a determinative in words associated with positions of authority.

One of the finer statues of the several hundred of the goddess **Sekhmet** that were originally provided within the temple of Mut in Asher at Karnak. The lioness-headed goddess wears a crown of royal uraei, most others on the site had a plain head-dress, and she holds an ankh flat on her lap with her left hand. New Kingdom.

teristic. Osiris had the epithet 'great sekhem, who dwells in the Thinite nome'. In the shape of a fetish the sekhem could also become a manifestation of divine power. It was a staff of office, with a pair of eyes carved into the upper part. This emblem of might was indigenous to Abydos; it is repeatedly found in connection with Osiris and became the emblem par excellence of the mortuary god Anubis as seen, for example, on his divine standard next to the jackal.

Sekhmet Together with her husband Ptah and her son Nefertem, Sekhmet made up the Memphite triad. Her name meant 'the mighty one', her nature being that of a goddess of war. She accompanied the king to battle and was often described as his mother. She spread terror everywhere; the henchmen of Seth and even the serpent Apophis succumbed to her. Sekhmet was represented as a lioness or as a woman with a lion's head, her weapons were arrows 'with which she pierces hearts' and a fiery glow emanated from her body. The hot desert winds were regarded as the goddess's hot breath. She was connected with the fire-spitting uraeus of the king and thereby became the 'eye of Re'. With the rise of Thebes to the position of royal residence the local goddess Mut was honoured anew by becoming merged with Sekhmet. Amenhetep III had numerous lion-headed statues of Mut-Sekhmet set up in the area of the temple of Mut in Asher, which lay just outside the temenos wall to the south of the great temple of Amun at Karnak, Thebes. Sekhmet was also regarded as the one 'great of magic' whose knowledge of sorcery gave her a place in the service of healing.
See illustration on p. 105

Selket One of the four protector goddesses of coffins and canopic jars. Her symbol was the scorpion, which she often wears on her head. She was particularly identified with the sun's scorching heat. References to her, often together with her three protector-goddess companions (Isis, Nephthys and Neith), are frequent in the Book of the Dead and in the earlier Pyramid Texts, e.g. 'My mother is Isis, my nurse is Nephthys, she who suckled me is the *Sh3t-Hr* cow, Neith is behind me, and Selket is before me' (No. 1375).

Sepa *see* CENTIPEDE

Serapeum The extensive underground galleries discovered by Auguste Mariette in

Four graceful figures of goddesses stood guarding the canopic chest in the 'Treasury' in the tomb of Tutankhamun. Three of them seen here wearing their appropriate hieroglyph on their head are, from left to right: Neith, Isis and **Selket**. XVIII Dynasty, *c.* 1354 BC. From the tomb of Tutankhamun, no. 62 in the Valley of the Kings, Thebes, Egyptian Museum, Cairo.

1850 at Sakkara, Memphis, that were the burial place of the sacred Apis bulls. Two dozen huge granite and basalt sarcophagi of sacred bulls were found in alcoves opening off the main galleries, and they weighed up to 70 tons each. Most of them had been smashed and robbed in antiquity although one burial of the reign of Ramesses II was intact. Hundreds of stelae invoking the aid and protection of the Apis were found let into the walls of the entrance by devotees. An avenue of sphinxes flanked the dromos approach (they are mentioned in Strabo), and there was a half circle of statues of Greek poets and philosophers nearby.

Not far away Professor W. B. Emery discovered in 1970 the Iseum, the galleries that were the burial place of the cow mothers of the Apis. *See also* APIS.

Serapis A composite god introduced into Egypt under Ptolemy I (304–282 BC). As a god of the corn supply Serapis wore a corn modius on his head and assimilated the characteristics of Osiris, the Apis bull of Memphis and the Hellenistic elements of Zeus, Aesculapius and Dionysus. He was also a god of the underworld. His main cult shrine was the great Serapeum temple at Alexandria, a centre of learning famous for its library. The cult of Serapis spread widely throughout the Greek and the Roman world; a temple dedicated to him is recorded in an inscription from York (*Eburacum*) in Roman Britain, but his popularity was overshadowed by Isis, the other Egyptian deity whose worship also went far outside the boundaries of Egypt.

Serekh A rectangular frame that contained the pharaoh's name. In the earliest dynasties it was the usual way of writing the name before the oval cartouche came into use. Later, the pharaoh's 'Horus' name was written within the serekh while his prenomen and nomen were written in the cartouche. At the bottom of the serekh frame is a design of recessed panelling such as is found used for the brick-built façades of the early dynastic tombs and on Old Kingdom false doors. It is often referred to as the 'palace façade'. The rectangle with its pattern symbolized a building, probably the royal palace or the pharaoh's tomb, seen simultaneously in plan and section. Surmounting the serekh was the falcon of Horus, hence the pharaoh's 'Horus' name. In the Second Dynasty at one point the religious supremacy of Seth is indicated

Bust of **Serapis** with traces of gilding from the Serapeum at Alexandria. He has the usual modius, or corn measure, on his head, appropriate as a god of the corn supply. In classical times Egypt was the granary of Rome, and the corn fleet sailed annually from Alexandria to Ostia, the port of Rome at the mouth of the Tiber. Graeco-Roman Museum, Alexandria.

by his animal standing on top of the serekh. The pharaoh Sekhemib changed his 'Horus' name to the 'Seth' name of Peribsen, with the consequent change in the animal surmounting his serekh. His successor obviously reconciled the difference of religious opinion, adopted the name Khasekhemwy ('the two Powers have appeared'), and had both the Horus falcon and the Seth animal standing on his serekh.

Serpent, snake The snake was one of those animals whose symbolism showed the most glaring contrasts. Its speed, slithering beauty, its mystery and dangerousness evoked worship and abhorrence. As a chthonic animal the snake was one of the life-creating powers, for example, the four female members of the Ogdoad bore snake heads and Amun appeared as a primeval deity in the form of the serpent Kematef. When the corn was brought in and wine was pressed an offering was made to the harvest goddess, Thermuthis, who was serpentine in form or was depicted as a woman with a serpent's head. Furthermore, the demons of time and certain divisions of time were in the same form; the two-headed snake Nehebkau appears in the book of the netherworld, Amduat, and the attendant vignettes. The most important serpent deity was Wadjet, whose sacred animal, the uraeus wound herself round the king's diadem.

The Apophis serpent was the most preeminent of evil powers as the opponent of Re. On the other hand, the snake Mehen, 'the coiled one', was a helpful attendant of the sun-god on his journey through the realm of night. She was represented draped in many coils above the cabin. The Book of the Dead crawls with serpent demons, sometimes winged, rearing up or standing on legs, spitting fire or armed with a knife. Lastly, the snake, because it sloughs its skin, became a symbol of survival after death, as in Chapter 87 of the Book of the Dead. The snake biting its own tail was a symbol of the boundlessness of the sea because of the reptile's connection with the profound. The second shrine of Tutankhamun shows the head and feet of a mummiform god, perhaps Ptah, wound about by such a snake; this alluded to the ocean above and below which was so significant in myth. In the eleventh hour of Amduat the serpent with many coils, 'the one who surrounds the world' symbolized the pre-cosmic primeval state in which the sun-god, and all creation with him, renewed itself each night.

Stele of King Djet (or Uadji) with his name represented by a snake within a **Serekh** surmounted by the Horus-falcon. From Abydos. I Dynasty, *c*. 3000 BC. Louvre Museum, Paris.

Seshat The goddess of writing, Seshat, was venerated under the epithet 'she who is foremost in the house of books'. On the founding of a temple either she or her priest established the ground-plan with a measuring cord, hence she was also the 'lady of builders'. Her most important function was that of recording the regnal years and jubilees which were allotted to the king. Her head-dress resembled a seven-pointed star surmounted by a bow, or was perhaps a crescent moon often crowned by two falcon feathers. She usually held a palm leaf in her hand and often wore a panther skin over her dress.

Seshmu A god mentioned from the Old Kingdom onwards, often as a god of perfume. He appears in the Book of the Dead in chapters concerned with escaping from nets, 'As for this peg which is in my hand, it is the shin of Seshmu' (Chap. 153), and as a provider (Chap. 170): 'Seshmu is with thee; he gives thee of the best of fowl'.

Seth One of Seth's commonest epithets was 'great of strength'. In one Pyramid Text (No. 1145) it states that the king's strength is that of Seth. The god appeared as the Upper Egyptian companion of the Lower Egyptian royal god, Horus. The Egyptian king himself as 'heir to the two brothers' united the 'offices of Horus and Seth'. Seth fought the Apophis serpent while standing in the bows of the solar barque. There are also representations in which this ship was pulled by Seth animals instead of the usual jackals. During the Hyksos Period Seth was regarded as the chief god, and in the Nineteenth and Twentieth Dynasties he was the patron of the Ramessides, hence the royal name Seti.

Seth always represented one half of the ancient Egyptians' dualistic world view. He was regarded above all as lord of the desert and appeared as the opponent of the vegetation god, Osiris. The latter was compared to the life giving Nile, whilst the cruel sea was thought to be a manifestation of Seth. Seth's chthonic features contrasted with those of the sky god, Horus. It was through his breath that worms emerged from inside the earth; he was also the lord of metals, iron ore being called the 'bones of Seth'. When Osirian beliefs took over, Seth came partially to be outlawed. Horus rose to become the avenger of his father and in the ensuing battle Seth lost his testicles and Horus an eye, but Thoth 'calmed the white-hot anger' in the hearts of the combatants (Book of the Dead, Chap. 183). Besides the ass and the antelope, the

Two **Serpents** drawn on the wall of the tomb of Seti I have the names of the goddesses Nephthys and Isis inscribed in front of them. They are the royal uraeus snake, and one carries the White Crown of Upper Egypt on its back, the other the Red Crown of Lower Egypt. XIX Dynasty, c. 1310 BC. Tomb no. 17 in the Valley of the Kings, Thebes.

Statuettes of the god **Seth** are rare. This very fine example has its kilt inlaid with silver. It has, however been adapted into a more acceptable god, Amun, by cutting off the long ears of Seth and replacing them by the ram's horns of Amun. XXII Dynasty, 945–715 BC. Ny Carlsberg Glyptotek, Copenhagen.

pig, hippopotamus, crocodile and fish were regarded primarily as Sethian animals. As lord of the desert, as a 'red' god, Seth also became lord of all non-Egyptian lands. During the time of foreign rule, especially after the Assyrian invasion, he thereby became a national enemy and a figure symbolic of all evil.

Seth animal The god Seth was worshipped in the form of an animal, the species of which cannot be ascertained. Attempts at identification range from an aardvark to an okapi and from a canine to an antelope. According to the earliest representations it seems to bear the strongest resemblance to an ass. Its characteristic features were the erect, arrow-like tail and square-topped, pricked ears. In earlier times Seth was depicted anthropomorphically but with the head of his animal surmounted by the double crown. The eleventh Upper Egyptian nome, the emblem of which was the Seth animal, may have been the actual centre from which the worship of Seth spread. At any rate the authority of the ruler of the Upper Egyptian nomad hunters was embodied in this animal, whilst he was a symbol of evil among the agricultural inhabitants of the Delta. The god as well as his animal were identified with the desert.

Shabti, Shawabti *see* USHABTI

Shadow The shadow was an essential part of a man next to his body and soul. In New Kingdom tombs the black shadow of the deceased was often shown leaving the tomb in the company of the soul bird (the *ba*). In the Book of the Dead (Chap. 92) the text runs, 'Open a way for my soul (that of) one who controls his feet that it may see the great god within the barque of Re (on the day) of counting souls.'

In a very hot land 'shadow' could also become a symbolic word for 'protection', which was represented by the sign of the shade-giving flabellum. It was said of the king that a divine shadow rested on him. 'Shadow of Re' was the term for the holy places of the sun-god at Amarna.

Shemset girdle In the Archaic Period gods and kings, for example Narmer and Djoser, wore as a symbol of power a girdle with an apron of pendant beads which was called shemset. It is likely that this term derived from a mineral of the same name which was found in the land of Shemset on the eastern edge of the Delta. The 'lord of the shemset' was Sopdu who wore such a girdle, and this, it has been suggested, was an apron of narrow strips of leather.

Shield The shield was an ancient symbol of protection. Hemsut, the deity of protection and destiny who also appeared as the female counterpart of the '*ka*', possessed one as an emblem and head-dress. Above the shield were two crossed arrows. The whole was similar to the nome sign of Sais and the cult symbol of Neith, the goddess of war. The other symbol of Neith, a rectangle with two hook-like structures, may have been nothing more than a stylized shield with arrows crossed behind it. According to another explanation it represented two bows in a case, which sometimes served as the goddess's head-dress, as on the canopic chest of Tutankhamun. Besides the battle-axe, the shield was an attribute of the protective war-god Reshef who was adopted from Canaanite-Phoenician peoples during the New Kingdom. The shield of black crocodile leather served as the ideogram for 'black'.

Ship Ancient peoples generally regarded the ship as a symbol for transition from one stage of life to another; the 'voyage of life' was a familiar concept. For the Egyptians the ship was also an imaginative expression for a passage, above all for the interim phase between life and death. In Middle Kingdom tombs models of ships were one of the most common items of burial equipment. These not only made it possible for the deceased to have a pleasant journey as he did when alive, but beyond this they were certainly linked with the notion of safeguarding the journey to the west and into the other world. It was the dead person's wish to travel 'in the barque of Re' (Book of the Dead, Chap. 136), which was a symbolic expression for walking in the light.

Shrew Proof has been found for the shrew's religious significance not only among classical authors, for example, Plutarch, but in the mummies of these animals, in the depictions intended for devotional purposes and in written references in religious literature. Bronze figurines of shrews were often covered with solar symbols; the winged scarab, the winged disc, falcon and uraeus. The characteristic feature of the shrew is the long muzzle and elongated nose. In statues the legs were always parallel, so that when represented standing the animal contrasts to the ich-

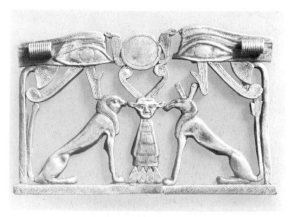

Chased back of an electrum pectoral. The central part of the design is the head of the goddess Bat, with cow ears and horns. Flanking her are, on the right, the **Seth animal** with its characteristic pricked-up ears and arrow-like tail. Opposite it, on the left, is Horus as a hieracosphinx. The two rival gods appear here as heraldic supporters representing Upper and Lower Egypt. Above them are a pair of wedjet-eyes flanking a sun-disc supported by royal uraei. Said to come from Dahshur. XII Dynasty, *c.* 1991–1786 BC. Eton College, Windsor.

A typical Ptak-**Sokar**-Osiris figure, mummiform, with a head-dress incorporating ram's horns, sun-disc and plumes. The base upon which it stands is a miniature sarcophagus with four hawks with sun-discs on their heads on it. Many of these figures were hollow and had copies of the Book of the Dead secreted in them; others are solid and have hollow pedestals in which there might be a small papyrus or even a fragment of mummified remains. XXVI Dynasty, 664–525 BC. British Museum.

neumon with its striding gait. In Letopolis the shrew was worshipped as the sacred animal of Horus. According to E. Brunner it could have represented the dark side of the god of light because its typical nature was that of a poor-sighted subterranean mouse, whilst the ichneumon which lived above ground represented the clear-sighted aspect of Horus. In a demotic magical papyrus the magician changed himself into a shrew, 'm'm, dwelling in Letopolis so that he might then cause blindness and death. On the north wall of the burial chamber of Ramesses VI in the Valley of the Kings the shrew may be found in scenes concerning the rebirth of the sun during the night.

Shu According to an ancient myth Shu had issued as breath from the nose of the primeval god. Together with his sister-wife Tefnut, goddess of moisture, Shu, the air, embodied the forces necessary to life. Moreover, Shu was identified with the sun and Tefnut with the moon. The offspring of both were the sky goddess, Nut and the earth god, Geb. The fatherly air god lifted the vault of the sky on upraised arms thereby separating it from the earth, thus he assumed the function of a support of heaven. Because Atum was identified with Re, Shu became 'son of Re', and it was in this manner that Shu who fought on the sun's behalf was given a lion's head; otherwise he was depicted in human form with his hieroglyphic sign, a feather, on his head.

Sistrum This musical instrument used in worship could have had its origin in the custom of picking a bundle of papyrus flowers in honour of the goddess Hathor and shaking them in a ritual movement to produce a rushing sound. Two types of sistra may be distinguished, the hooped sistrum and the naos type. The latter may be traced back to the Old Kingdom. The handle of the naos sistrum terminated in a Hathor head on which stood a naos surmounted by two or three lugs of curled wire, an allusion perhaps to the goddess's horns. Often a uraeus appeared within the naos. The three or four rods with attached rattles often had serpent form in both types of sistrum. The hooped sistrum was also a cult symbol of Hathor. Texts of songs describe how the goddess used her instrument as a medium for imparting blessings. The sistrum also entered the cult of Amun and later that of Isis.

The sound of the sistrum was supposed to scare off the powers of darkness. According to Plutarch the metal loops of the hooped sistrum, which was predominant in later times, represented the world-encircling orbit of the moon, the two opposing faces of Hathor symbolized Isis and Nephthys as life and death, and the four rods alluded to the four elements.

Sobek *see* SUCHOS

Sokar Sokar was worshipped on the desert edge at Memphis. He may have begun as an earth and fertility god. During his festival a stone, his cultic image perhaps, was dragged across the fields in a barque fixed to a sledge whilst many people followed after with garlands of onions round their necks. Sokar became a mortuary god because his cult centre was near the necropolis. Deities were equated with the king, therefore, Sokar assumed the form of the divine falcon and was then represented sitting on a stone. In the Pyramid Texts (No. 620) the god had already been brought into relation with Osiris. According to the fifth hour of Amduat, Sokar, 'he who is upon his sand', dwelt in a secret cavern, called Imhet, the netherworld. He was shown anthropomorphically but with a falcon's head. In the Late Period he became conflated with Ptah and Osiris as Ptah-Sokar-Osiris.

Solar barque The conception of the heavens as a stretch of water corresponded to the mythical image of the barques in which heavenly bodies travelled. The most important was the solar barque 'which gleamed of gold'. Actually there were two vessels, the day barque, Mandet, and the night barque, Mesektet. There are scenes in which the gods of the east and west standing at either end of the barque, replace the solar disc by the ram-headed sun-god. Both barques were equated with the eyes of the lord of heaven. This and the other symbolism, which sprang from the association between west and the right side, and east and the left side, led to the following concept: the night barque travelling in the west, i.e. the netherworld, the land of the dead and darkness, became the right eye, the sun and, therefore, Mandet; the day barque rising in the east became the left eye, the moon and, therefore, Mesektet. Models of sun barques have been found in tombs; these were an expression of the desire to take part in the voyage of Re. It is not certain that the two boats discovered near the pyramid of Khufu (Cheops) at Giza were meant to be solar barques, as is usually alleged. They may only have been a means whereby the deceased could achieve his desire to travel to all the great national feasts of the gods.

Nun, the god of the primeval waters, lifts up the **Solar barque** of the sun-god Khepri, represented as a scarabeus beetle accompanied by seven gods; the one at the back by the steering oars has a falcon head. Book of the Dead of the priestess Anhai, XX Dynasty, *c.* 1100 BC. British Museum.

Solar eye The sun was regarded as the right eye of the sky and according to the conception of ancient nomads, he was thought to be a falcon hovering over the earth. The sun, therefore, became first of all the right eye of the falcon god, Horus, but was soon addressed as the 'eye of Re'. The solar eye was not only part of Re's body but could also appear as an independent entity. There are myths in which the eye leaves Re either to carry out his orders, for example, to destroy his enemies, or out of anger against him. One tale links both of these aspects; it tells how the solar eye returned to Re, having carried out its mission, only to find that another eye had grown in its place. The god reconciled himself with the solar eye by placing it on his brow as the uraeus. According to one Pyramid Text (No. 705), the solar eye was the disc between the horns of Hathor.

Sopdu The god worshipped in the twentieth Lower Egyptian nome was called Sopdu. His hieroglyphic sign and his cult image showed him as a crouching falcon. Otherwise he appeared anthropomorphically with a crown of two falcon feathers and a shemset girdle. In the Pyramid Texts he was often mentioned in connection with the teeth of the deceased, a fact which is unexplained. Outside his own nome Sopdu gained significance as god of the frontier and of the east. He was already linked to Horus in the Middle Kingdom, which led in the New Kingdom to the name Har-Sopdu.

Sothis The dog star Sirius that was deified as a goddess and shown as a woman with a star on her head. The 'Sothic cycle' was one of 1460 years, the time that it took for the Egyptian calendar to correct itself since the adjustment made by a leap year every fourth year was not known; therefore the error was cumulative. It is known that in the reign of Antoninus Pius in AD 139 the rising of Sothis coincided with the first day of the Egyptian New Year (it was also commemorated by a special coin being issued at Alexandria that referred to the event). From this it is possible to work backwards and calculate and therefore date quite closely documents or events that make reference to a Sothic rising in earlier years.

Sothis, represented as a large dog, was later associated with Isis; she is shown riding side-saddle on the animal as Isis-Sothis on some of the coins from the Greek Imperial (i.e. Roman colonial) mint of Alexandria.

Soul The complete person of a human being was composed of a *ka*, an ankh and a *ba* in addition to the body, name and shadow. The former three concepts have still not yet been clearly defined and took on various meanings during the course of Egyptian history. The *ba*, a bird with human head, corresponded most closely to the Greek concept of the psyche, whereas the ankh, which was represented in hieroglyphic script by the crested ibis, simply meant transfiguration. The gods also possessed this state of being and also those who had been 'transfigured' through the mortuary cult. In one Pyramid Text (No. 474), the text runs, 'the spirit is bound for the sky, the corpse is bound for the earth'. Whenever the word for 'soul' appeared in Egyptian writings, one normally had the *ba* in mind, as when one spoke of the jackal-headed souls of Nekhen (Hierakonpolis) or the falcon-headed souls of Pe (Buto). These beings were all meant to embody the spiritual individuality of the dead kings of those towns.

Spear of Horus *see* HORUS

Sphinx The Egyptian sphinx was, with only a few exceptions in representations of some queens of the Middle Kingdom, shown as male, unlike the Greek sphinx which was female. Also, the Egyptian sphinx was viewed as benevolent, a guardian, whereas the Greek sphinx was invariably malevolent towards people. The sphinx was the embodiment of royal power, often shown smiting the king's enemies, or the king himself being represented as a victorious sphinx trampling on his foes. The latter was especially popular on pieces of royal jewellery, the inscribed bases of scarabs, and also occurs on some of the wooden parade shields from the tomb of Tutankhamun. Avenues of sphinxes flanked the ceremonial entrances to numerous temples; at Karnak they were ram-headed in honour of Amun, at Luxor they have the head of the pharaoh Nectanebo.

The most famous sphinx is the great Sphinx at Giza which formed part of the funerary complex of Khafre (Chephren) of the Fourth Dynasty, *c*. 2540 BC. It lay beside the pharaoh's Valley Temple and the covered causeway that led from it up to the Pyramid Temple against the east face of the pyramid. Over 240 ft in length, the Great Sphinx was sculpted from an outcrop of limestone and represented Harmachis, 'Horus of the Horizon', the sun-god at his rising in the east. Its features were probably a portrait of Khafre. A stela between its paws records how

The god **Sopdu** as god of the frontier, carrying a tall *was* sceptre, an axe, and an ankh.

The Great **Sphinx** of Giza with the pyramid of Khufu (Cheops) in the background. Its face was probably a portrait of Khafre (Chephren), the builder of the Second Pyramid at Giza. Between its paws can be seen the top of the stela erected by Tuthmosis IV. IV Dynasty, *c.* 2540 BC.

prince Tuthmosis was out hunting one day and fell asleep in its shadow. The Sphinx appeared to the prince in a dream and promised him the throne of Egypt if he would clear away the sand that encumbered and almost completely buried his body. The prince did this, and reigned as Tuthmosis IV (1425–1417 BC).

Spiral Spirals had already been painted on pots in prehistoric times as early as the Nagada II culture. Some researchers suppose that these alluded to coiled snakes, therefore the wavy lines on the same vessels would be creeping snakes. From the Middle Kingdom onward scarabs bore the royal name not in a cartouche but more often within a spiral or wreath of interlocking bands. In this case the symbolic significance is certain: the spiral line was the line of life, hence it is also found on amulets. The spiral symbolized the cycle of growth and decay, of birth and death and therefore had more than a merely decorative purpose in the tomb paintings of the Middle and New Kingdoms.

It was probably not by chance that the head-dress of the goddess Meskhenet consisted of a rod or stem ending in a double spiral, for she was a personification of the birth brick and was also thought to be present at the hour of the judgment of the deceased. It is quite likely that a magical effect and symbolic meaning were ascribed to the spiral, twisted lock of the divine child, the young Horus.

Spittle Spittle was an ancient mythical symbol of animation throughout the East; for example, the spittle of the Babylonian god Marduk was called 'spittle of life'. The Egyptian primeval god, Atum, produced Shu and Tefnut out of his own person. The former was the air-god, i.e. breath, and Tefnut was moisture, i.e. spittle. The mouth was the mythical place of birth in this case: 'I spewed it forth from my mouth. I emitted Shu and spat out Tefnut'. There is a reference in the Pyramid Texts (No. 199) according to which the earth came forth from the spittle of the beetle-shaped primeval god, Khepri. The healing power of spittle was displayed in the saga of the lost and rediscovered eye of the moon which Thoth spat out and 'filled' again, which was an image of the waxing of the moon.

Staircase In ancient Egypt ladders and steps were early symbols of ascension; one representation shows Osiris as 'the god at the top of a staircase', thus symbolizing his resurrection from the dead. The Step Pyramid of Djoser at Sakkara probably represented a staircase which was to facilitate the ascension of the dead king to heaven. The primeval hill, which appeared from the primeval ocean thus initiating creation, could be shown as a flight of stairs. One amulet given to the deceased represented a staircase, which was certainly a symbolic expression of the primeval hill and the hope for new life that was connected with it. In the 'Book of the Dead' (end of Chap. 153) the text runs that the deceased 'ascends on this ladder which his Father Re made for him'.

Standards Evidence of emblems fixed to wooden poles can be found back into prehistoric times. Ships with standards were depicted on the pottery and in rock drawings of the Nagada II culture. The meaning of individual emblems has not been totally explained. Three types of standard from historic times may be distinguished:

1 Divine standards with the images and symbols of individual deities. These played an important role in the royal cult and were carried by priests in procession. When a king died, he was accompanied on his last earthly journey to the tomb by divine standards; these were called the 'following of Horus'. The standard of Wepwawet, the divine 'opener of the ways' was borne first, then there followed a crouching falcon, a standing ibis, a striding Seth animal, the so-called Min emblem (which was a double-pointed harpoon), and the so-called Khonsu emblem. Two interpretations of the last are worthy of mention: a) that it was the cushion on the royal throne, and b) a container for the king's placenta which was regarded as a twin of the ruler.
2 Nome standards consisting of a portable support and the nome sign which usually represented the image of the nome deity or, according to the beliefs of that time, an object imbued with power.
3 The military standards which likewise carried divine images as a symbol of might and victory.

Stars The stars were the 'inhabitants of the Duat', the netherworld, the realm of the dead. They were, therefore, called the 'followers of Osiris', who was lord of the dead. According to an ancient belief the dead lived on in the stars and it was the pious wish of many Egyptians to be allowed to continue living as a small lamp among the constellations of night, hence coffins were adorned with stars. The circumpolar stars received special respect for they were regarded as the 'imperishable ones' because they never sank in the west. The main southern constellation of Orion was called Sah by the Egyptians and had already been early equated with Osiris. In religious texts one finds the notion of the sorrowing Isis in the form of Sirius (Sepdet in Egyptian, corrupted to Sothis in Greek) following Orion, the 'glorious soul of Osiris'.

The circuit of the sky was arranged into thirty-six sections, each of these being under the sign of a star or constellation which the Egyptians called 'servant stars' and the Greeks decans. The decans were often termed 'the thirty-six gods of heaven' and each ruled over a ten day period. Graeco-Egyptian magical papyri expounded upon the mutual connections between the constellations on the one hand and metals, animals and parts of the body on the other, which may have been adopted from the Middle East as a result of Persian rule. It may be that the inspiration for the zodiac ceiling formerly in the temple of Dendera (now in the Louvre) also came from that area.

Stone The Egyptian who was so closely linked to the powers of nature saw the hardness and immutability of stone as a manifestation of absolute being in contrast to the unstable and fragile existence of man. In their untouchable state, mountains, rocks and stones were a symbol of durability, of eternity: if the human body decayed, the sculptured stone image and its engraved name would guarantee survival. Obelisks and also statues of gods and kings were supposed to be monolithic as, for example, the colossi of Memnon (Amenhetep III) which stand to a height of 15 m. above their bases at Thebes.

As an image of durability and immovability the stone could also become a symbol of the sacred centre where all planes of existence, heaven, earth and the netherworld met. Heliopolis possessed a cone-shaped stone fetish called the Benben which was venerated as the place where the primeval god was manifest. A stone cone adorned with ornamentation and divine images was set up in the temple of Amun at Napata. In the oasis of Siwa the god whom the Greeks called Ammon, i.e. Amun, had a cone-shaped stone symbol which one Roman author compared to an 'umbilicus', the navel of the earth.

Suchos The name of the god Suchos, which is tentatively rendered in Egyptian as

The crocodile god **Suchos** was especially revered at the Ptolemaic temple of Kom Ombo (shared in a dual dedication to Haroeris). He appears frequently in high relief wearing an atef crown and carrying a *was* sceptre and an ankh. Many mummified crocodiles have been found in the area about the temple.

Stele of Niai and his wife Isis kneeling in adoration before the **Sycamore** tree from which the goddess holds forth a table laden with food and pours water for them to drink. At the foot of the tree are two *ba* (soul) birds. New Kingdom, 1600–1100 BC. Kestner Museum, Hanover.

Sebek, means 'crocodile'. His chief cult centres were Crocodilopolis in the Fayum and Kom Ombo in Upper Egypt. The Twelfth Dynasty which had its residence in the Fayum especially favoured the cult of Suchos in honour of whom the Thirteenth Dynasty rulers incorporated his name in theirs, as in Sebek-Hetep, 'Suchos is merciful'. Representations of crocodiles which carry a falcon's head adorned with the double crown were founded on the relationship between Suchos and the royal god, Horus. A further identification with Re led to a form of the crocodile with the solar disc on its head. The Greeks generally depicted Suchos as Helios with a halo of rays and the attribute of a crocodile in his hand. Suchos was understandably a god of the water; the Nile issued from his sweat, he 'made the herbage green' and therefore took on a somewhat Osirian character.

Sun The versatility and complexity of Egyptian thought is displayed in solar symbolism. There were many cross connections between the sun, which manifested the symbol and the sun-god who possessed it. The name of the luminary was Re, the same as that of the god it personified. There were other solar deities besides him. Herakhty and Khepri in the form of the winged beetle were gods of the morning sun whilst Atum and the ram-headed gods, for example, Khnum, were regarded as lords of the evening sun.

The three most important images of the day sun were the beetle in the morning, the sun-disc, Re himself, at midday and the ram in the evening. In the Late Period the sun was given a form peculiar to each hour of its daily course: in the first and second hours it was a child, in the seventh a monkey shooting an arrow, i.e. a ray of light, and in the eleventh and twelfth hours it was an old man, often with a ram's head, leaning on a stick. A representation in the tomb of Ramesses IX shows the crocodile for the first and second hours, the basis of this concept being that the sun-god appeared each morning in crocodile form from the celestial ocean. Other solar animals were the falcon, lion and griffon. The image of the rising sun was often connected with the horns of the celestial cow, with two sycamores, the ankh or the djed-pillar.

The connection of the sun-god to the lotus was already established in the Old Kingdom and it can be seen to be the same until the end of the Late Period. He was the 'child . . . who rose from the lotus' (Nefertem). On one Twentieth Dynasty ostracon the sun-god bears the name 'great lotus who appeared from Nun'. According to an inscription at Dendera the king presented a lotus as an offering to 'him who rose in the lotus', thus referring to Horus. Solar symbolism and ideas concerning the cosmos were mutually linked in the offering of flowers.

Supporters of Heaven A god usually appeared as a supporter of the sky. In this connection the premier god was Shu 'who uplifts the sky with the breath of his mouth'. It was he who supported the body of the sky goddess Nut with his powerful arms. Another god who supported the sky was Heh, represented kneeling with upraised arms. Anhur, Onuris, the god of Thinis appeared in his function of supporter of the sky and was often equated with Shu in the New Kingdom. The sky, which was personified as a goddess, was supported by Iuwenmutef, i.e. 'pillar of his mother'. In the Book of the Dead (Chap. 172) it was said that he bore Re on his shoulders. On the outer face of the western side wall of the temple at Edfu one relief shows the king, with head-dress and bull's tail, holding up the sky with his arms. In this case the ruler appears as the upholder of the laws which were laid down by heaven and without which world order would collapse. According to one Pyramid Text (No. 389) the sky was supported by a djed-pillar.

Swallow The deceased wished to be transformed into a swallow along with other sacred birds such as the falcon, heron and phoenix, so that he might 'go forth by day unrestrained through any gate in the god's domain and assume his form as a swallow' (Book of the Dead, Chap. 86). We know that the swallow was worshipped as a sacred animal in the Theban area from the Eighteenth Dynasty. According to Plutarch it was in the form of this bird that Isis had fluttered around the pillar containing Osiris' coffin.

Sycamore 'Twin sycamores of turquoise' (Book of the Dead, Chap. 109), stood at the eastern gate of heaven from which Re went forth each morning. Pyramid Text No. 916, speaks of 'yonder tall sycamore in the east of the sky, quivering of leaves, on which the gods sit'. The sycamore became a celestial tree and was regarded as a manifestation of the sky goddess, Nut, who was to 'shield' the dead Osiris and 'rejuvenate his soul among her branches'. Sycamore leaves had amuletic significance since they 'helped one gain many good things'. A Late Egyptian cult centre of the crocodile god, Suchos, was called the 'House of the Sycamore'. One of the most ancient tree cults was that of 'Hathor, Lady of the Sycamore', near Memphis.

T

Tatjenen A very early earth god of the Memphite region represented as a bearded man wearing a crown composed of two feathers and a solar disc above a pair of ram's horns. He was later identified with the creator-god Ptah of Memphis.

Taweret, Taurt Since the Archaic Period this hippopotamus goddess was represented standing upright with human arms and legs. She held the attribute of the *sa* in her hands and sometimes also the ankh or a torch, the flame of which was supposed to expel typhonic forces. Taweret was especially helpful to women during childbirth. The image of this protective goddess was attached to beds, head-rests and cosmetic articles but she is also found in the vignettes of the 'Book of the Dead' and even in temple reliefs.
See illustration on page 120

Tefnut Tefnut and her brother, Shu, were produced by the primeval god Atum from his own body. Thus duality emerged with them from the primordial unity and the sexual cycle was begun. In Leontopolis these siblings were identified with the lion worshipped there. Because of the assimilation of Atum into Re, Shu and Tefnut became the children of the sun-god and were regarded as the eyes of the 'lord of all'. At first Tefnut was equated with the lunar eye but through various mythological cross-connections she became the solar eye and then the uraeus. Tefnut, therefore, bore the epithet 'lady of flame' and 'the uraeus on the heads of all the gods'. In Buto, Shu and Tefnut were worshipped in the form of the flamingo-like 'children of the Lower Egyptian king', which was a mythical image for sun and moon. *See also* CREATION LEGENDS.

Tekenu Earlier representations of the Tekenu show a crouching man wrapped in skin from head to toe. In later representations it consists of a pear-shaped bundle or a naked man with arms and legs drawn in. The Tekenu may be described as a ceremonial

The hippopotamus goddess **Taweret** standing holding a torch, ankh and *sa* before a laden table of offerings. Behind her the cow goddess Hathor emerges from a hill with a menat around her neck; at the base of the hill is a small tomb with a pyramidal top. Book of the Dead of Ani, XIX Dynasty, *c.* 1250 BC. British Museum.

object which had its origin in archaic burial customs, c.f. the animal-skin wrap and crouching posture. The significance attached to the Tekenu in historic times has not been completely explained but some have thought it to be a symbol representative of human sacrifice. Others see it merely as a substitute image of the deceased which as a kind of scapegoat was to confront the uncanny powers of the next world. It is more probable that the Tekenu was regarded as a manifestation of the deceased through which the transfigured person would be led to places with promise of life, such as the 'lake of Khepri' and the 'town of the animal skin'.

Temple The regulations which priests gave with regard to temple building were attributed to the god, Thoth. The very earliest form of the temple consisted of a reed hut with a curved roof and a forecourt, at the entrance of which stood two poles each with a triangular pennant which was later the written sign for god. The flags which in the ensuing era were placed on the four or more flagpoles had apotropaic significance. The pylons on the national temple at Karnak had eight poles. In the Archaic Period the 'god's house' (*hwt ntr*) was characterized by having three parts, sanctuary, hypostyle hall and courtyard. The square or rectangular sanctuary held the shrine with the divine image. The cult symbols such as the divine staff and mace and often the portable barque were kept here. Subsidiary chapels for attendant deities were grouped around the inner sanctuary. The further away from the sanctuary the other temple rooms were, so the broader and higher they became and the more they were open to the light. The pylons were described as Isis and Nephthys who 'raise up the sun-god who shines on the horizon'. The whole temple was a symbol of the world in stone. The lower part represented the earth from which the three plants, papyrus, lotus and palm sprouted in the form of columns. The ceiling was the vault of heaven and was therefore painted with stars and divine birds. *See also* OBELISK; PYLON.

Theoris *see* TAWERET

Thigh The bull's thigh which was presented as an offering was used as the written sign denoting the human arm and was a symbol of strength. In the southern part of the Delta the second nome was given the name and emblem of 'thigh', a fact which proves that this sign already had forceful significance in early times. The following was said of one area in the next world 'the thighs of the spirits which one sees here are seven cubits long'. Besides the knee the thigh was a mystic organ of birth for Khepri was called 'he who appears on the thigh of his mother'. There are also representations in which the god in beetle form creeps up the thighs of his mother Nut, the sky, in order to push the sun's disc before him.

Thoth In early times various traditions had already coalesced in the figure of Thoth. The meaning of his name, Djehuty in Egyptian, is uncertain. The god's ibis head suggests that the Delta was his home, for the fifteenth Lower Egyptian nome had the ibis as its emblem. In historical times the chief cult centre of Thoth was at Hermopolis in Middle Egypt where he merged with Hedj Wer, the indigenous baboon deity, and assumed the latter's form. Thoth was lord of the moon. In the Late Period he acquired the epithet 'silver Aten'. One cannot tell whether or how far the Egyptians saw the moon as a crouching baboon analogous to our 'man in the moon' and the curved beak of the ibis as a symbolic allusion to the lunar crescent.

One myth relates that Thoth sprang from the head of Seth after the latter had inadvertently swallowed the semen of Horus. The cosmic background to this image was clearly explained by the Egyptologist H. Bonnet: 'Through the power of the god of light the full moon breaks forth from Seth, the power of darkness.' This connection with the moon made Thoth the 'lord of time' and 'reckoner of years', hence the fact that his attributes were often a writing palette or a palm leaf. As the god who invented writing he was the protector of scribes. Thoth was occasionally described as the tongue or heart of Re. As a protector of Osiris he also became a helper of the dead, which led to his identification with Hermes by the Greeks.

Tomb The tombs of kings and high officials consisted of three essential parts:

1 The tomb chamber, the actual resting place, described by the Egyptians as the 'House of Gold'. From the end of the Fifth Dynasty texts from mortuary literature (the Pyramid Texts) were written on the walls whilst spells concerning the sky goddess Nut were written on the ceiling or nearby. In later times the tomb was conceived of as being an earthly reflection of the night sky, hence the fact that the ceiling was often painted with stars. In the New Kingdom a special brick

Both the ibis and the baboon were sacred to the god **Thoth**. Here, in his baboon aspect, he is represented as the patron of scribes; he was the god of writing as well as of learning and lord of the moon. On his head is the sun's disc and the lunar crescent. The scribe squats before him, an open papyrus roll on his lap and his palette resting on his left knee. From Amarna. XVIII Dynasty, *c.* 1365 BC. Egyptian Museum, Cairo.

The Valley of the Kings at Thebes has the greatest concentration of famous **Tombs** in the world. Virtually all the pharaohs, and some queens, of the New Kingdom were buried here, starting with Tuthmosis I in *c.* 1512 BC. The valley is dominated by a natural pyramid, the 'Lady of the Peak' and was the domain of the goddess Mertseger, 'She who loves silence'. In this view the entrance to the tomb of Ramesses VI is on the right (Tutankhamun's is just out of sight immediately to the right in front of it); further along the path on the right is the tomb of Horemhab, last king of the XVIII Dynasty.

with a symbol and a magic spell was set in each of the four walls of the tomb chamber: a djed-pillar in the west wall, a ushabti in the north wall, a jackal to the east and a torch to the south.

2 The cult chapel, in which the deceased partook of earthly existence in a magical way and where he was provided with food and drink. In Predynastic and Early Dynastic burials there were real food cupboards. In later times the deceased was supposed to obtain possession of all the necessities of life through the magic power of pictures. The sacrificial meal was represented in every detail on the wall of the tomb. Agricultural scenes like seedtime and harvest, grape gathering and bread baking also served this purpose. Incense was burnt in the cult chamber in honour of the deceased. The symbolic connection between the living and the dead was represented by the false door.

3 The *serdab* (arabic for 'cellar') consisted of one or several walled-up rooms in which the statue of the deceased was set up. Slits at eye level enabled the statue to hear the prayers and to inhale the incense.

See also BURIAL.

Tongue According to the Memphite theology the world came into being through the word of Ptah. The heart and tongue were his organs of creation, for it was by means of his tongue that he brought to life that which he had conceived in his heart. A similar conception is found in connection with the god Atum. The tongue was the symbol of will made manifest and of authoritative utterance and, therefore, has certain similarity to Hu, the personification of command. Intelligent Thoth was regarded as the tongue of the creator god, hence he bore the name 'tongue of Re, lord of the divine words'.

Transformation Osiris was the *nb ḫprw* (*neb kheperu*), 'lord of forms' who concealed all modes of being in his person. He manifested himself in the waters of the Nile, in the sprouting corn and in the trees reaching to the sky. Osiris, himself, was the symbolic figure of 'to die and come into being', whose dead body produced new life, i.e. his son, Horus.

The dead person's ability to transform himself was a symbolic expression of his immortality and references to this are found again and again in the 'Book of the Dead', as when the deceased is called 'cosmic egg' (Chap. 54), or 'golden falcon' (Chap. 77), as 'sacred lotus' (Chap. 81), or as 'royal phoenix' (Chap. 83). Space and time were no longer applicable to the deceased. 'I am today. I am yesterday. I am tomorrow. Undergoing my repeated births I remain powerful and young.' As a lion-headed Re, he took possession of his celestial inheritance.

Tree It was said of various deities that they had come forth from the tree, for example, Horus from the acacia, Re from the sycamore and Wepwawet from the tamarisk. According to Theban temple inscriptions the sky goddess Nut bore Osiris under the *kesbet* tree, the species of which cannot be identified. Tree cults were widespread in the Nile valley. An acacia was venerated in Heliopolis in which 'life and death were decided' and it, therefore, paralleled the ished-tree. Herybakef, 'he who is beneath his moringa tree', was a god worshipped on the desert edge at Memphis, who had already merged with Ptah in the Old Kingdom. Two Upper Egyptian nomes had sacred trees as their signs, the 'sycamore nome' which split into the thirteenth and fourteenth nomes and the 'tree nome', No. 20 or 21.

The connection between tree and man is shown in the Tale of the Two Brothers. It tells of the heart of Bata which rested in a

Ramesses-Nakht, High Priest of Amun, kneels to present a small shrine upon which are represented the Theban **Triad** of Amun, Mut, and their son Khons. From Karnak. XX Dynasty, *c.* 1120 BC. Egyptian Museum, Cairo.

cedar blossom. When the tree was felled Bata had to die. As the living found refreshment in the shade of a tree so the souls of the dead also alighted on trees. Again and again images show female tree spirits, who were thought of as the sky goddesses Nut or Hathor, giving water and handing fruit to the soul of the deceased who was in bird form. The tree, especially the date palm and sycamore, was therefore a tree of life. Whoever drank of the water of life and ate of the celestial fruits lived on after death. Many tombs had their sacred tree. Every tomb of Osiris, which many towns possessed, had a grove which was regarded as the resting place of the god's *ba*. Right by the sarcophagus was a tree symbolically indicating the resurrection. In texts it was stated that the 'sarcophagus becomes green'.

Triad Several groups of triple deities existed at certain major cult centres in ancient Egypt. The trio is usually composed of father, mother and son. It is possible that the triads grew up as a convenient theological answer and means of bringing together deities of an area previously separate. The major triads were extremely powerful, or more correctly, their priests were. At Thebes there were Amun, Mut and Khons (their moon-god son); at Memphis, Ptah, Sekhmet and Nefertem; at Edfu, Horus, Hathor and Harsomtus (Horus the Younger); and at Elephantine there were Khnum, Anukis and their daughter Satis. The most widely worshipped of the triads, Osiris, Isis and Horus (later Harpocrates) did not have a joint cult centre or specific area of worship but individual major shrines at Abydos, Philae and Edfu respectively.
See illustration on p. 125

Two Ladies *see* NEKHBET; WADJET

The **Uch**, a staff fetish associated with the cult of Hathor.

U

Two figures of the Nile god Hapi tying the lotus and papyrus together around lungs and windpipe signifying the **Union** of the Two Lands. XIX Dynasty, 1304–1237 BC. Egyptian Museum, Cairo.

Uch The staff fetish worshipped in Cusae was represented by a papyrus stem crowned with two feathers. 'Uch' meant 'the pillar' and was, among other things, a symbol of the support of heaven. All that one can be certain of is that the Uch belonged to the cult of Hathor.

Udjat-eye *see* WEDJAT-EYE

Union The historical event of the 'Union of the Two Lands' (Upper and Lower Egypt) was symbolically repeated at each coronation and was at the same time a recourse to the primeval age. It was, indeed, the gods themselves who 'placed all plains and mountainous countries under the feet' of the ruler. The symbolic representation of unity usually decorated the side panels of the throne of royal statues. In the form of their heraldic plants, the Upper Egyptian reed, or lotus, and the Lower Egyptian papyrus, the two lands were twined together by Horus and Seth around the hieroglyphic sign *sma*, i.e. unity, which consisted of lungs and windpipe. The king took his place above this entwined motif either enthroned, seated or represented by his cartouche. Seth was occasionally replaced by the god Thoth. The national goddesses Wadjet and Nekhbet could be represented flanking the ruler.

Uraeus The Greek word Uriaos may have originated in the Egyptian world meaning 'she who rears up'. The uraeus was the serpent which the king wore on a diadem or from the Middle Kingdom on his crown. It was represented as a rearing cobra with inflated hood. This emblem, worn on the head, it has been suggested, may be traced back to the forelock worn by the tribes of ancient Libya. Others regard the snake as the symbolic animal of the prehistoric kingdom of Buto in the Delta, the goddess of which, Wadjet, sat in uraeus form on the king's brow. The uraeus was a symbol of kingship and was, therefore, worn by the royal gods Horus and Seth. The flame-spitting serpent which averted all evil was defined as the fiery eye of the sun god, Re. Because Hathor was thus equated with the sun god she could therefore be evoked as the uraeus as, for example, in the Coffin Texts. Tefnut in her special function as goddess of fire, Wepes, wore a uraeus on her head.

Ushabti The ushabti is a figurine, usually mummiform, which was placed in the tomb to carry out the necessary work in the next world which the deceased might be called upon to do. The linguistic origin of the word is of unknown meaning; from the end of the Old Kingdom the Egyptians themselves interpreted it to mean 'answerer'. Whenever the deceased was called in the next world to sow the fields, to fill the canals with water and to carry the sand of the east to the west, or vice versa, i.e. to clear the canals of their silt, the ushabti was supposed to reply, 'Here

The royal cobra, the **Uraeus**, was the protector of the pharaoh and was supposed to spit fire at his enemies from its place on his forehead. This uraeus, and the vulture with it, were not found on the diadem but lower down on the mummy of Tutankhamun. The vulture (as the goddess Nekhbet of El Kab) signifies Upper Egypt, and was found on the pharaoh's right, south, side. The uraeus (as the goddess Wadjet of Buto) symbolizes Lower Egypt, and was found on his left, north, side. The body lay east to west with the head to the west, so each creature was laid on its appropriate side of the pharaoh. They have been replaced on the royal diadem, into which they slot. XVIII Dynasty, *c.* 1354 BC. From the tomb of Tutankhamun, no. 62 in the Valley of the Kings, Thebes. Egyptian Museum, Cairo.

am I'. In order that the figure could come alive magically to carry out these tasks the best examples were inscribed with the name of the deceased and a version of the Sixth Chapter, the Ushabti Chapter, of the Book of the Dead: 'O thou ushabti, if the Osiris N. is counted off to do any work that is to be done yonder in the god's domain – lo, obstacles have been set up for him yonder – as a man to his duties, thou art charged with all these tasks that are wont to be done yonder, to cultivate the fields, to irrigate the shores, to transport sand of the west or of the east. "I will do them; here I am", shalt thou say.'

In the early New Kingdom the ushabti was provided with little model tools of the implements required, a hoe, pick and basket. Later the objects were painted or moulded onto the figures. Ushabtis usually held a hoe and/or pick in their hands and they had a basket for carrying sand on their back. Some were also supplied with water bottles. It is thought that generally 365 'answerers' were placed in the tombs of those that could afford their provision, one for each day of the year. There were also 'reis' ushabtis, overseers who were dressed in a civilian kilt and carried a whip in one hand; they seem to have been provided in a ratio of one to ten of the worker ushabtis. It is said that there were over 700 ushabtis in the tomb of Seti I, and there were at least 414 ushabtis in Tutankhamun's tomb.

V

A very fine painted wooden **Ushabti** figure of Ramesses IV. It is clearly inscribed with a version of the Sixth Chapter, the 'ushabti chapter', of the Book of the Dead, reading from right to left, and holds a hoe in each hand. XX Dynasty, c. 1141 BC. From the tomb of Ramesses IV, no. 2 in the Valley of the Kings, Thebes. Louvre Museum, Paris.

Vessel Pot, basin and vase are female symbols. According to psychologists they represent the mother's body, the receptacle of birth. In one Pyramid Text it says, 'NN has come forth from his pot having slept in his pot. NN appears in the morning'; morning was to the Egyptian an image of creation and birth. In the Tale of the Two Brothers the heart of the dead Bata which was in a pot awoke to new life. The sky goddess Nut wore a small round pot without handles as her distinguishing hieroglyph on her head. Nut was the vessel concealing the stars which came forth from the dark womb and returned to her. In the symbolically rich language of the Egyptians the coffin and the tomb chamber became Nut.

Female divinities were the guardians of the water of life, which was kept in pots without handles. Included in these were the four pots of Kebhut, the goddess of libation. Pots played an important role in the symbolism of offering therefore many reliefs on temple walls show the king presenting two round *nw*-pots of water, milk or wine to the gods.

Vulture The national goddess of Upper Egypt, Nekhbet, was either shown as a vulture or wearing the vulture head-dress. As a heraldic animal of Upper Egypt the vulture became part of royal symbolism. Next to the uraeus symbol of Lower Egypt on the forehead of the golden face mask of Tutankhamun there is the head of a vulture, and they are both also on his coffins. Images of vultures were part of the royal grave equipment and also found their way into the graves of private individuals. The vulture was the sacred animal of the goddess Mut whose chief cult centre was at Thebes and she was also represented in human form. In the Late Period the vulture was a symbol of the female principle and stood in juxtaposition to the beetle as the embodiment of the male principle. In one particular written device the combined images of the two animals served to denote the goddess Neith and also the god Ptah in whom, as creator deities, both sexes were united.

Vultures are also found painted on the underside of the ceiling blocks of temples, protecting with their outstretched wings the way to the sanctuary.

Wadjet The name of the goddess of Buto in the Delta meant the 'papyrus-coloured one', i.e. the 'green one'. This was, at the same time, a general term for the cobra which in uraeus form was the goddess's sacred animal. In later times the ichneumon was assigned to her. As a fire-spitting serpent Wadjet was equated with the royal uraeus and in the end became the 'eye of Re'. Because of her solar connections Wadjet could now and again assume a leonine head surmounted by the solar disc and uraeus. As a national goddess of Lower Egypt, Wadjet was the counterpart of the Upper Egyptian Nekhbet on whom she occasionally imposed her snake form. A rep-

resentation from the Late Period at Dendera shows both goddesses in snake form each sitting upon a papyrus plant. According to one Pyramid Text the papyrus plant was supposed to have emerged from the goddess. As the 'green one' Wadjet embodied the forces of growth. As the 'lady who is upon her papyrus . . . who brought up her son Horus in the Delta' she was assimulated with Isis. *See also* NEKHBET; NATIONAL SHRINE; URAEUS.

Was-sceptre In early times the *was*-sceptre was a type of fetish thought to contain the life-giving power of a dog or fox-like protective spirit. The *was* consisted of a staff forked at the bottom and terminating at the top in an animal head, probably that of a canid. It became a popular sceptre for the gods to hold and became a symbol of well-being and happiness. Into the Middle Kingdom wooden *was*-sceptres were placed in the tomb with the deceased so that he might enjoy divine prosperity. In later times friezes of objects on coffins were adorned with this symbol. A popular motif in all periods was the depiction of two *was*-sceptres framing an area containing a picture or inscription and supporting the sign for 'sky' on their heads. A *was*-sceptre decorated with a ribbon and feather was the emblem of the Theban nome and bore the name Waset.

See illustration on page 128.

Water The notion of the water of life was shown in the symbolism of purification, thought of not only in a superficial sense but also as supposed to provide divine grace. Water was the primeval matter which 'brought forth all things'. In the Tale of the Two Brothers the heart of Bata was awoken to new life by being steeped in cool water. Water was part of female symbolism. As the primeval waters, it fathered and gave birth and this was mythologically reflected in the couple Nun and Naunet who together formed an androgynous unity. During the festival of Osiris, celebrated in the month of Athyr, a model phallus, i.e. Osiris, and a vase full of water, i.e. Isis, were carried at the head of the procession. Both together these were symbols of reproduction and alluded in a sublimer sense to the imperishability of life. As a god of vegetation Osiris was himself regarded as lord of the waters of the Nile, whereas Isis manifested herself in the fertile land. The inundation which was so important to the Egyptians was, therefore, the union of the two poles of existence. In the mortuary cult the water used in libation was linked to the

Detail of a decorative frieze with **Was-sceptres** flanking ankhs standing on ornamented baskets. Temple of Hathor at Dendera. Ptolemaic period, after 116 BC.

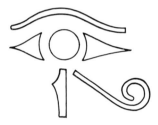

The **Wedjet-eye**, the left eye of Horus restored by Thoth, was a very popular symbol of protection.

idea of reanimation. As the 'efflux which issued from Osiris' water liberated one from the paralysis of death.

Wedjat-eye The lunar eye which, returned after Seth had stolen it, was healed by Thoth and then called 'the whole one'. It was a symbol of the power of the god of light, and therefore a popular amulet. Some wedjat-eyes had an arm carrying the ankh or the papyrus staff, symbol for 'to flourish'. The wedjat-eye was also used as a protection against the evil eye. From the late Old Kingdom two wedjat-eyes were placed on the door recesses of tombs; these had apotropaic significance as did those on Middle Kingdom coffins and New Kingdom sarcophagi.

Weighing of the Heart The scene showing the ceremony being carried out was one of the most popular of those represented in copies of the Book of the Dead from the beginning of the New Kingdom. (There is a rare occurrence of it in relief carving on the wall of a chapel in the small Ptolemaic temple at Deir el-Medineh.) The deceased is shown being introduced into the Hall of Judgement by the jackal-headed god Anubis. His, or her, heart is placed in one of the pans of a balance to be weighed against the feather of Truth, Maat. Anubis then adjusts the plummet whilst Thoth, generally shown as ibis-headed, writes down the verdict. Nearby a demon, the 'Eater of Hearts', a grotesque composite of crocodile, lion and hippopotamus, waits expectantly for a verdict against the deceased, when the heart will then be thrown to it. Whilst the weighing takes place the deceased recites the Negative Confession, addressed to the 42 gods who sit in the Hall, denying all sorts of heinous crimes as well as some more mundane ones. Upon a satisfactory verdict the deceased is then led by Horus before Osiris who sits in a pavilion at the end of the Hall of Judgement, attended by Isis and Nephthys. The deceased is presented as one 'true of voice, justified' and a suitable candidate to be admitted into the joys of the netherworld.

Wepwawet The god of Lycopolis was represented in the form of a standing canid, a jackal or a wolf. The name Wepwawet means 'opener of the ways' and may have been connected to the idea of proceeding victoriously into battle. His attributes of mace and bow are in accordance with the god's warlike character. As the 'leader of the gods' Wepwawet with his standard opened the royal procession, and not only did the jackal-like deity precede the king but also Osiris. Speculative considerations concerning the Osirian mysteries and the symbolism of resurrection contained therein were an impetus to many Egyptians to place the following wish on stelae: 'to behold the beauty of Wepwawet during the procession'. Lastly, the god in the form of two standards went before the funeral procession at Abydos and once placed by the tomb, he kept watch over the dead.

White Because of its lack of colour white became expressive of earthly omnipotence, a means of denoting sacred things like the 'White Wall', i.e. Memphis, the 'white chapel' and the 'white unguent'. White sandals were mentioned in connection with cult ceremonies. White was the colour of purity and sanctity. The white vulture, the symbolic animal of the Upper Egyptian patroness, Nekhbet, hovered over Pharaoh's head. White became the chief heraldic colour of Upper Egypt, the crown of which was described as 'white', although it actually consisted of green rushes. It is strange that Egyptians described the pupil of the eye as 'white', although this part of the eye is not at all that colour. It was also regarded as the colour of joy, thus the cheerful aspect of a person was described as being 'white'.

Willow The willow was sacred to Osiris because it had sheltered his coffin whilst his soul alighted upon the tree as a phoenix. During the festival of 'raising the willow' in the temple the gods promised the king that the fields would be fertile and the trees flourishing. In the New Kingdom the ceremony of 'raising the willow' was also adopted into the cult of Amun.

Wind Whereas other peoples tended to personify the wind, the Egyptians only saw it as a secondary manifestation of the divine. The north wind, which brought refreshment to the hot desert came from the 'throat of Amun' and it was said of Hathor, the 'lady of the sycamore', that the 'breath of life' proceeded from her lips. The lord of the air was actually Shu who preserved all that existed in his 'form of the pleasant north wind'. The deceased also needed air; in the Coffin Texts he was equated with Shu and power 'over the four winds of heaven' was given him. A popular motif in Amarna art was the fluttering ribbons on wigs and girdles which was an illusion to the effective power of the creator god which manifested itself in the wind.

Scene of the **Weighing of the Heart** in the Hall of Judgment. On the right the owner of the papyrus looks on anxiously as her heart is weighed against the feather of Truth (Maat). Anubis adjusts the plummet and Thoth writes down the result. The repugnant 'Devourer of Hearts' also waits, but in vain. Book of the Dead of the priestess Anhai, XX Dynasty, c. 1100 BC. British Museum.

Wine According to one myth Isis became pregnant and bore her son, Horus, by savouring grapes, an allusion to the cosmic vine and by extension to the tree of life. According to another version Osiris was said to have been conceived in the same parthenogenic way. In the Pyramid Texts (No. 820) Osiris was 'Lord of wine'. In a Greek magical papyrus wine was addressed as part of the vegetation god's substance. The god of the wine press Shesmu handed this life-giving drink to the deceased but he pulled the heads of sinners down and crushed them in his press. It was said of Horus that he drank blood of his enemies as he drank wine.

Winged disc An ancient conception of heaven held that it was the wings of a falcon stretched out over the world. A drawing on a First Dynasty comb shows the solar barque, together with the Horus falcon, on a pair of wings thus symbolizing heaven. From the Fifth Dynasty onwards a sun disc was placed between the pair of wings, hence the image of heaven became a solar symbol. Originally the winged disc belonged to the god Behdet whose epithet was 'he with coloured plumage' and who had already merged with Horus at an early date. With that, Behdeti began to assume the role of Horus who was identified with the king. The two uraei which surrounded the solar disc towards the end of the Old Kingdom were a part of royal symbolism; there are New Kingdom representations in which the snakes' heads wear the Upper and Lower Egyptians crowns respectively. After the New Kingdom the winged disc appeared as a symbol of protection above temple doors and at the top of stelae.

Word The Egyptians believed that creative power resided in each word. The demiurge, Ptah, called into being by means of his word that 'which the heart thought and the tongue brought forth'. It was said of Re that the gods came into being through his word. The word of Re became personified as Hu who accompanied the sun god, together with Sia, the embodiment of perception. The king, too, however, was comparable to Hu and Sia as the earthly representative of god. Creation by virtue of divine utterance was closely connected with the concept of the magical power of names. Whoever knew a demon's true name was able to raise him, and by doing so dangerous animals and illnesses were banished. The magic became more effective when the sorcerer identified himself with a particular deity. The curse was a special form of linguistic magic which could be strengthened by means of symbolic rites, thus the names of enemies were written on clay tablets or figurines that were smashed with a club.

Wreath After the New Kingdom 'wreaths of justification' were given to the deceased and to their ruler in the netherworld, Osiris. This custom was a symbolic expression of the innocence proved by the court of the next world. Such wreaths were wound around the diadems of dead kings and later became a general feature of the decoration on mummy cases. One text draws a comparison with the wreath, which Osiris received from the primeval god Atum as a token of his triumph over his enemy. The wreaths were to a large extent made of the leaves of olive trees. *See also* FLOWERS.

Chronological Table
Select Bibliography
Index to the illustrations
Photographic acknowledgments

Chronological Table

Date	Political History	Cultural and Religious History
Predynastic Period 5th–4th millennium BC	5000–4000 Neolithic Period 4000–3000 Late Neolithic Period Confrontation of Upper Egyptian nomads and Lower Egyptian agriculturalists	Totemism Local gods in plant and animal form Veneration of the Mother Goddess Geometric ornamentation of the Neolithic Period
Archaic Period *c.* **3100–2686**	Supremacy of Buto, Hierakonpolis and Abydos I–II Dynasty, Thinite Period. Pharaohs of 1st Dynasty: Narmer, Menes, 'Scorpion', 'Serpent', etc.	Anthropomorphization of deities Personification of the forces of nature Pharaoh the incarnation of the universal god, Horus First written symbols on monuments of Hierakonpolis Cosmetic palettes (*cf.* Narmer palette) Apogee of ivory carvings
Old Kingdom *c.* **2686–2181** *c.* 2613–2494 *c.* 2494–2345 *c.* 2345–2181	III–VI Dynasty Capital: Memphis III Dynasty: Zoser IV Dynasty; Snefru, Khufu, Khafre, Menkaure V Dynasty: Sahure, Unas VI Dynasty: Pepi II	Theological system of Heliopolis (sun-god Re, local god Atum), and of Memphis (local god Ptah) Pharaoh the son of Re Construction of pyramids from III Dynasty; Step Pyramid of Zoser, *c.* 2670, first great stone building in the world. Great Sphinx of Giza Pyramid Texts appear Sun temples open to the sky Reliefs in mastaba tombs of nobles

Date	Political History	Cultural and Religious History
First Inter-mediate Period c. **2181–2133**	VII–X Dynasty Herakleopolitan Period Disintegration of the Kingdom into Herakleopolitan and Theban territories	Doctrine of the *ba* Increasing development of concept of the deceased becoming Osiris Abydos becomes centre of Osiris worship Concept of judgement of dead Early Coffin Texts Decline of sculpture
Middle Kingdom c. **2133–1786** c. 1991–1786	XI–XII Dynasty XI Dynasty: name of most important pharaohs Mentuhotep Thebes becomes the capital XII Dynasty Royal Residence at Fayum Names of most important pharaohs: Amenemhet, Senusret	Rise of cult of Amun in Thebes Later Coffin Texts Tombs of nomarchs at Beni Hasan Earliest extant obelisk at Heliopolis (On) First appearance of so-called cube-statues and Hathor columns Mortuary temple (the 'Labyrinth') of Amenemhet III at Hawara, Fayum
Second Inter-mediate Period c. **1786–1567** c. 1650–1567	XIII–XVII Dynasty XIII Dynasty: name of most important pharaoh Sebekhetep XV Dynasty: foreign rule under Hyksos. Royal Residence at Avaris in Delta XVII Dynasty: indigenous to Thebes	Infiltration of Syrian deities begins; Seth equated with Baal, national god of the Hyksos Last royal tombs in pyramid form
New Kingdom c. **1567–1085** c. 1567–1320	XVIII–XX Dynasty XVIII Dynasty Amenhetep I	Amun becomes the national god Book of the Dead placed in the tomb

Date	Political History	Cultural and Religious History
	Tuthmosis I Queen Hatshepsut Tuthmosis III conquers large areas of Syria Amenhetep III	Mortuary temple of Hatshepsut at Deir el-Bahari Extension of temple of Amun at Thebes (Luxor) Colossi of Memnon—seated statues of Amenhetep III
	Amenhetep IV = Akhenaten Royal Residence at Amarna	Naturalistic art of the Amarna Period. Akhenaten, the 'heretic king', introduces belief in the Aten; almost monotheistic in conception
1320–1200	Tutankhamun XIX Dynasty Seti I Ramesses II (treaty with Hittites) New Royal Residence at Pi-Ramesse	Mortuary temple of Seti I at Abydos Rock-cut temples at Abu Simbel
1200–1085	XX Dynasty Ramesses III (the last great display of power) to Ramesses XI	Mortuary temple of Ramesses III at Medinet Habu
Transition to Late Period 1085–656	XXI–XXV Dynasty	Animals once regarded as manifestations of the god are now seen as objects of veneration *per se*, especially the bull, crocodile and cat (increasing importance of goddess Bastet)
c. 1085–935	XXI Dynasty Royal Residence at Tanis	
	In Upper Egypt the theocracy of Amun	Many representations of figures holding a naos
935–730	XXII Dynasty: founded by the leaders of Libyan mercenaries in Bubastis XXIII and XXIV Dynasty in Sais (also Libyan)	
c. 750–656	XXV Dynasty: Ethiopian (Nubian) foreign rule	Remarkably realistic statuary
671	Assyria conquers Egypt	

Date	Political History	Cultural and Religious History
Late Period 664–332	XXVI–XXX Dynasty	Increasing tendency towards organized religion and theological speculation leads to a popular counter-movement with magical concepts and practices So-called Serapeum for burial of Apis bulls built by Psamtik I at Sakkara
664–525	XXVI Dynasty: Psamtik I and Necho reside at Sais in the Delta	
525–404	XXVII Dynasty: foreign rule of Persians	
404–343	XXVIII–XXX Dynasty Last indigenous princes in the Delta Nectanebo I	
332	Egypt conquered by Alexander the Great	
Ptolemaic (Hellenistic) Period 332–30	Capital of the Ptolemies at Alexandria	Ptolemy I introduces the Graeco-Egyptian hybrid deity Serapis. Cult of Isis spreads outside Egypt Temple of Khnum at Esna
31	Battle of Actium	Temple of Horus at Edfu Temple of Hathor at Dendera
30	Cleopatra VII commits suicide, Egypt becomes part of the Roman Empire under Augustus	Double temple of Suchos and Haroeris at Kom Ombo

Select Bibliography

ALLEN, T. G. *The Book of the Dead or Going Forth By Day: Ideas of the Ancient Egyptians concerning the Hereafter as expressed in their own terms.* Chicago, 1974.

——*The Egyptian Book of the Dead: Documents in the Oriental Institute Museum at the University of Chicago.* Chicago, 1960.

BLEEKER, C. J. *Egyptian Festivals. Enactments of Religious Renewal.* (Studies in the History of Religions, Supplements to *Numen* XIII). Leiden, 1967.

——*Hathor and Thoth.* Leiden, 1973.

BONNET, H. *Reallexikon der ägyptischen Religionsgeschichte.* Berlin, 1952.

BREASTED, J. H. *Development of Religion and Thought in Ancient Egypt.* New York, 1959.

BUDGE, E. A. W. *The Book of the Dead.* 2nd ed. rev. and enlarged. London, 1928.

——*Egyptian Magic.* London, 1901.

——*From Fetish to God in Ancient Egypt.* London, 1934.

——*The Gods of Egypt, or Studies in Egyptian Mythology.* London, 1903.

——*The Liturgy of Funerary Offerings.* London, 1909.

——*The Mummy: A Handbook of Egyptian Funerary Archaeology.* 2nd ed. Cambridge, 1925.

——*Osiris and the Egyptian Resurrection.* 2 vols. London, 1911.

BUHL, M. L. 'The Goddesses of the Egyptian Tree Cult,' *Journal of Near Eastern Studies* 6 (1947), 80–97.

ČERNÝ, J. *Ancient Egyptian Religion.* London, 1952.

CLARK, R. T. *Myth and Symbol in Ancient Egypt.* London, 1959, repr. 1978.

DAVID, A. R. *A Guide to Religious Ritual at Abydos.* Warminster, 1980.

——*Religious Ritual at Abydos.* Warminster, 1973.

DERCHAIN, P. 'Mythes et dieux lunaires en Egypte', *Sources orientales* 5 (1962), 19–68.

ERMAN, A. and H. Grapow. *Ägyptisches Handwörterbuch.* Darmstadt, 1961.

FAIRMAN, H. W. *The Triumph of Horus.* London, 1974.

FAULKNER, R. O. *The Ancient Egyptian Coffin Texts.* 2 vols. Warminster, 1973, 1977.

——*The Ancient Egyptian Pyramid Texts.* 2 vols. Oxford, 1969.

FRANKFORT, H. *Ancient Egyptian Religion.* New York, 1961.

GARDINER, A. *Egyptian Grammar.* 3rd ed. revised. Oxford, 1957.

GRIFFITHS, J. G. *The Conflict of Horus and Seth from Egyptian and Classical Sources: A Study in ancient mythology.* Liverpool, 1960.

HABACHI, L. *The Obelisks of Egypt.* London, 1978.

HARRIS, J. R. (ed.). *The Legacy of Egypt.* 2nd ed. Oxford, 1971.

HELCK, W. 'Die Mythologie der alten Ägypter', *Wörterbuch der Mythologie,* vol. 1, 313–406. Stuttgart, 1965.

——and E. OTTO. *Kleiner Wörterbuch der Ägyptologie.* Wiesbaden 1956, 2nd ed. 1970.

JAMES, T. G. H. (ed.). *An Introduction to Ancient Egypt.* London, 1978. (revised and enlarged edition of *A General Introductory Guide to the Egyptian Collections in the British Museum.* London, 1964).

KEES, H. *Bemerkungen zum Tieropfer der Ägypter und seiner Symbolik.* Nachrichten der Akademie der Wissenschaften in Göttingen. Phil.-hist. No. 2, 1942.

——*Farbensymbolik in ägyptischen religiösen Texten.* Nachrichten der Akademie der Wissenschaften in Göttingen. Phil.-hist. No. 11, 1943.

——*Der Götterglaube im alten Ägypten.* 2nd ed. Berlin, 1956.

——*Totenglaube und Jenseitsvorstellungen der alten Ägypter.* 2nd ed. Berlin, 1956.

——'Herz und Zunge als Schöpferorgane in der ägyptischen Götterlehre', *Studium Generale* 19 (1966), 124–6.

LESKO, L. *The Ancient Egyptian Book of Two Ways.* Berkeley, Calif. 1972.

LICHTHEIM, M. *Ancient Egyptian Literature.* 2 vols. Berkeley, Calif. 1973, 1975.

LURKER, M. 'Hund und Wolf in ihrer Beziehung zum Tode', *Antaios* 10 (1969), 199–216.

——'Der Baum im Alten Orient. Ein Beitrag zur Symbolgeschichte', in *In Memoriam Eckhard Unger. Beiträge zu Geschichte, Kultur und Religion des Alten Orients.* Baden-Baden, 1971. 147–75.

——'Zur Symbolbedeutung von Horn und Geweih unter besonderer Berücksichtigung der altorientalisch-mediterranen Kulturen', *Symbolon* 2 (1974), 83–104.

MONTET, P. 'Hathor et le papyus', *Kêmi* 14 (1957), 92–101.

MORENZ, S. *Egyptian Religion*. London, 1973.

MURRAY, M. A. *The Splendour that was Egypt*. London, 1949.

OTTO, E. *Egyptian Art and the Cults of Osiris and Amon*. London, 1968.

PETRIE, W. M. F. *Amulets*. London, 1914.

PIANKOFF, A. *La création du disque solaire*. Bibliothèque d'etude 19. Cairo, 1953.

——and N. RAMBOVA. *Mythological Papyri*. 2 vols. New York, 1957.

——*The Wandering of the Soul*. Princeton, 1974.

PLUTARCH. *De Isis et Osiride*.

POSENER, G. *A Dictionary of Egyptian Civilization*. London, 1962.

REYMOND, E. A. E. *The Mythical Origin of the Egyptian Temple*. Manchester, 1969.

RINGGREN, H. 'Light and darkness in ancient Egyptian religion', in *Liber amicorum. Studies in honor of C. J. Bleeker*. Leiden, 1969. 140–50.

ROEDER, G. *Die ägyptische Religion in Texten und Bildern*. 4 vols. Zurich, 1959–61.

SALEH, A.-A. 'The so-called "Primeval Hill" and other related elevations in ancient Egyptian mythology', *Mitteilungen des Deutschen Archäologischen Instituts, Kairo*, 25 (1969), 110–20.

SCHÄFER, H. *Principles of Egyptian Art*. Edited and with an epilogue by Emma Brunner-Traut. Oxford, 1974.

SETHE, K. 'Das Papyrusszepter der ägyptischen Göttinnen und seine Entstehung', *Zeitschrift für ägyptische Sprache und Altertumskunde* 64 (1929), 6–9.

——*Übersetzung und Kommentar zu den altägyptischen Pyramidentexten*. 6 vols. Glückstadt, 1939–62.

SHORTER, A. W. *The Egyptian Gods: A Handbook*. London, 1937, repr. 1979.

SIMPSON, W. K. (ed.). *The Literature of Ancient Egypt: An anthology of stories, instructions, and poetry*. New ed. New Haven, 1973.

WAINWRIGHT, G. A. *The Sky Religion of Egypt*. London, 1937.

ZABKAR, L. V. *A Study of the Ba Concept in Ancient Egyptian Texts*. Studies in Ancient Oriental Civilization 34. Chicago, 1968.

Index to the illustrations

g=god; gds=goddess; k=king, pharaoh.

Photographic acknowledgments

The author and publishers are grateful to the following persons and institutions for permission to reproduce illustrations on the pages indicated.

Ashmolean Museum, Oxford: 61, above; 64; 102.

Trustees of the British Museum: 25; 29; 32, above; 36, below; 37; 43, below; 51; 62; 68, above; 69; 77; 90; 99, below; 112; 113; 120.

Peter A. Clayton: 24; 27; 28; 32, below; 33; 35, above; 38, above; 42, below; 43, above; 47; 56; 57; 58; 65; 68; 71; 78; 80; 85; 86; 87; 92; 93; 96; 99, above; 103; 104; 105; 107; 108; 109; 117; 124; 125; 128; 129.

Egypt Exploration Society, London: 36, above.

Egyptian Museum, Cairo, Service de Antiquités: 49; 50; 70; 121; 123.

By permission of the Provost and Fellows of Eton College, Windsor: 111.

Griffith Institute, Ashmolean Museum, Oxford: 40; 73, above; 84; 106.

L. V. Grinsell, OBE, FSA: 15.

Professor Max Hirmer, Hirmer Verlag, Munich: 17; 18; 42, above; 97; 122.

Kestner Museum, Hanover: 118.

Foto Marburg: 63.

Metropolitan Museum of Art, New York: 11; 53; 61, below; 88; 101.

Musée d'Art et d'Histoire, Geneva: 67.

The Ny Carlsberg Glyptothek, Copenhagen: 110.

Royal Scottish Museum, Edinburgh: 66.

Soprintendenza alle Antichita (Egitologia), Turin: 54.

The line drawings were drawn by Garth Denning, and the map by Mrs Hanni Bailey.